The Social Play Record

of related interest

Creative Expressive Activities and Asperger's Syndrome
Social and Emotional Skills and Positive Life Goals for Adolescents
and Young Adults
Judith Martinovich
ISBN 1 84310 812 7

Social Awareness Skills for Children
Márianna Csóti
ISBN 1 84310 003 7

My Social Stories Book
Carol Gray and Abbie Leigh White
Illustrated by Sean McAndrew
ISBN 1 85302 950 5

Revealing the Hidden Social Code
Social Stories™ for People with Autistic Spectrum Disorders
Marie Howley and Eileen Arnold
Foreword by Carol Gray
ISBN 1 84310 222 6

**Social Skills Groups for Children and Adolescent
with Asperger Syndrome**
A Step-by-Step Program
Kim Kiker Painter
ISBN 1 84310 821 6

**Playing, Laughing and Learning with Children
on the Autism Spectrum**
A Practical Resource of Play Ideas for Parents and Carers
Julia Moor
ISBN 1 84310 060 6

Giggle Time – Establishing the Social Connection
A Program to Develop the Communication Skills of Children
with Autism, Asperger Syndrome and PDD
Susan Aud Sonders
Foreword by Andrew Gunsberg
ISBN 1 84310 716 3

**Assessing and Developing Communication
and Thinking Skills in People with Autism
and Communication Difficulties**
A Toolkit for Parents and Professionals
Kate Silver, Autism Initiatives
ISBN 1 84310 352 4

The Social Play Record

A Toolkit for Assessing and Developing Social Play from Infancy to Adolescence

Chris White

Jessica Kingsley Publishers
London and Philadelphia

First published in 2006
by Jessica Kingsley Publishers
116 Pentonville Road
London N1 9JB, UK
and
400 Market Street, Suite 400
Philadelphia, PA 19106, USA

www.jkp.com

Library of Congress Cataloging in Publication Data
White, Chris, 1953-
    The social play record : a toolkit for assessing and developing social play from infancy to adolescence / Chris White.
        p. cm.
    Includes bibliographical references and index.
    ISBN-13: 978-1-84310-400-1 (pbk. : alk. paper)
    ISBN-10: 1-84310-400-8 (pbk. : alk. paper) 1. Autistic children--Education. 2. Autistic children--Rehabilitation. 3. Social skills in children--Study and teaching. 4. Social interaction in children--Study and teaching. 5. Play therapy. I. Title.
    RJ506.A9W46 2006
    649'.154--dc22
                                                    2005034981

British Library Cataloguing in Publication Data
A CIP catalogue record for this book is available from the British Library

ISBN-13: 978 1 84310 400 1
ISBN-10: 1 84310 400 8

Printed and bound in Great Britain by
Printwise (Haverhill) Ltd, Suffolk

This work is dedicated to Norman, Amy, Fraser and Jenny, who challenged (and changed) my thinking.

Acknowledgements

I would like to acknowledge the collective interest, participation and commitment of the many individuals – parents, children, teachers, assistants and speech and language therapists throughout Lincolnshire – who contributed to the development and evaluation of the Social Play Record (SPR). Particular thanks are due to the staff and pupils at Gosberton House School for their involvement and sound criticism, and to Simone Glover of Lincolnshire Autism Outreach. I would also like to acknowledge my sponsors, Lincolnshire Autistic Society and Trent Focus Research and Development Group, for funding the research, and to thank Dr Glenys Jones, University of Birmingham Autism Unit, and Dr Jane Dyas, Trent R&D Group, University of Nottingham, for their advice and support. Finally, thanks are due to my husband for his love and forbearance.

Contents

PART 2: LINKS TO INTERVENTION   53

4. How it all Fits Together   55

Conclusion   71

Introduction

What is the Social Play Record?

The Social Play Record (SPR) is a practical tool for assessing and developing social play in children with social interaction needs, particularly autistic spectrum disorders. Social play is about relating to others, playing and making friends, important skills which have a long-term impact on adjustment in society, well-being and quality of life. The SPR is a step-by-step resource for assessing and developing these skills. It was designed and researched by education and health workers, in collaboration with parents and children.

The Social Play Record has two components: *Assessment* and *Links to Intervention*. The SPR Assessment identifies a child's social play skills and needs, considers others' perceptions and examines the contexts in which social play occurs. The 'Play Observation' section is a photocopiable resource for systematically recording the different kinds of social play in which a child engages and the key skills achieved at each stage. It is easily completed by those who know the child. The SPR Assessment also looks at the impact of opportunity, experience and attitudes on social play. There is a questionnaire for parents, a rating scale for practitioners, a peer preferences chart for children and a questionnaire on friends for self-evaluation. This range of measures makes the SPR flexible across ages, abilities and settings and helps to address issues of social inclusion. For a see-at-a-glance reference there is a summary sheet, a planning sheet, a profile of scores and a progress chart. Part 1, *User Guide for the SPR Assessment Resource*, explains how to use each section of the SPR Assessment, score the findings and plan intervention.

Part 2, *Links to Intervention*, relates assessment findings to intervention, providing a framework for developing social play. It offers practical guidance for what to work on, when and how. The sections in *Links to Intervention* correspond to those in the SPR Assessment. Approaches, strategies, activities and resources are recommended for each type of social play, together with small-steps component skills for target setting. Like the SPR Assessment, *Links to Intervention* addresses others' attitudes and the social play environment as well as looking at skill development.

Social play influences many areas of development, including cognitive, social, emotional, linguistic and cultural aspects. It is a primary route to social inclusion. Through social play, children develop an interest in social interaction and learn about the two-way process of communication. They learn critical social skills: how to engage with others, enjoy others' company, get along with others, build relationships and develop friendships. All children have a right to the knowledge, skills, opportunities and experiences that lead to such social competence. The Social Play Record offers systematic assessment and targeted intervention for children who experience difficulty with social interaction. It supports development and social inclusion by enhancing the understanding, knowledge and skills of families, children, practitioners and peers.

The SPR is a flexible tool. It spans development from early infancy to adolescence, providing an ongoing record of social play. It can be introduced at any age or stage within this developmental range. It is applicable for children of all learning abilities in any educational or social setting. It was originally designed for children with autistic spectrum disorders but has since proved helpful for children with other types of social interaction difficulty, including social care needs. It is an abilities-based assessment that focuses on emerging skills, strengths and interests, but it also records atypical variations within uneven developmental profiles so as to give a complete picture of social play.

Social play is an area of concern frequently raised by parents, teachers, clinicians and children with social interaction needs. The SPR is a collaborative tool, designed to encourage children, parents, carers and practitioners to work together, sharing their observations and complementary knowledge. The SPR is a structured tool. It pulls together qualitative and quantitative information in an easily accessible way, helping parents and practitioners to identify social play skills and needs, set intervention targets, and demonstrate progress. Its skills-based focus and small-steps structure readily translate into individual targets for education, therapy or care plans.

The SPR is founded on a comprehensive review of well-substantiated literature, reflecting empirical thinking and best practice. It has been evaluated over five years of field trials and shown to have theoretical validity, meeting the specifications for a functional assessment of social play, and practical application, addressing educational and clinical needs for assessment and intervention. The Social Play Record is acceptable within competency frameworks, meeting practitioners' requirements for evidence-based practice.

PART I

USER GUIDE FOR THE SPR ASSESSMENT RESOURCE

I

Overview of the SPR Assessment

The Social Play Record Assessment resource will help you to identify the stage at which a child is functioning in social play and which processes or skills to work towards. The SPR also examines the environments in which social play occurs. Play opportunities – settings, activities, play partners' attitudes and behaviour – affect a child's willingness and ability to participate. So, in addition to teaching social play skills explicitly, practitioners need to adapt play environments to enable access and inclusion for the child with social interaction difficulties.

The SPR Assessment provides an ongoing curriculum for social play, spanning development from early infancy to adolescence. The structured framework of the SPR will help you to analyse and interpret assessment information as it is recorded. When a child's skills and needs have been identified, it becomes easier to choose appropriate intervention targets, and to know what to look for when reading about an approach or strategy, to see if its components match the child's requirements.

The Social Play Record is not merely a checklist of skills. It uses five assessment measures to look at the different aspects of social play. Combining measures in this way is considered to give a more reliable and socially meaningful assessment than relying on one method alone. The five measures are:

- *the Home Comments Sheet*: a questionnaire for parents to communicate their observations, opinions and concerns

- *the Play Observation Sheets*: developmentally organised sheets for recording observations and knowledge of a child's social play

- *the Practitioner Rating of Peer Relationships*: a two-way rating with a friendship component

- *the Peer Preferences Chart*: looks at the perception and playmate choices of other children in the peer group

- *the Questionnaire about Friends*: a self-evaluation tool for assessing understanding of and interest in friendship.

Detailed instructions for using these five measures are set out in Chapter 2, How to use the SPR Assessment Resource.

There are a number of additional sheets to summarise the recordings of the SPR Assessment and to plan future actions and goals:

- *The Summary Sheet* profiles the assessment data, giving an overview of the child's social play skills and needs.

- *The Class Summary Profile* is an optional sheet to summarise types of play for a group of children.

- *The Planning Sheet* relates assessment findings to intervention goals. It specifies targets for social play and records the outcome of intervention. It links to education, therapy or care plans.

- *The Score Sheets* record quantitative information from the SPR Assessment.

- *The Profile of Scores Sheet* is an optional scoring system for summarising quantitative information from the SPR Assessment.

- *The Progress Chart* presents the quantitative information over time in a visual form, providing a see-at-a-glance chart of progress.

The initial assessment provides a baseline against which the outcomes of intervention and progress may be measured. The initial assessment takes the most time, after which the SPR can either be maintained as an ongoing record, with information added as it is obtained, or updated at intervals to fit in with education, therapy or care plans and the review process. Parents' information should also be updated. Worked examples of SPR assessments and scoring are included in Appendix 1.

The SPR Assessment addresses the three dimensions that are critical for the development of social play:

1. social skills, strategies and processes
2. cognitive diversity of play
3. social status, that is, evaluation of and by peers.

Assessment follows a developmentally organised schema based on key skills at each stage of social play (main headings) and the small steps (listed under the main headings) that lead towards mastery of that particular skill. The SPR covers several developmental periods from early social interaction to more complex group and friendship skills. However, it is important to recognise the co-existence of different types of play, the diversity of individual development, and the uneven developmental profile of many children with social interaction needs. Entries are made across the stages.

Most items in the SPR Assessment are skills, but some items describe the more unusual behaviours that children with autistic spectrum disorders sometimes engage in. This allows for sensitivity to the individual interests and needs of atypically developing children. It is particularly important to note *emerging* skills (present some of the time or prompted). Emerging skills offer a productive route to intervention. Collaborative practice underpins assessment on the Social Play Record. Sharing the assessment process helps practitioners and parents to gain a shared perspective and a more accurate picture of the child's strengths and needs. Collaborative practice is also important for successful intervention. It facilitates consistent management and promotes skill maintenance and generalisation.

2

How to use the SPR Assessment Resource

Home Comments Sheet

> Children achieve more when schools and parents work together. (DfES, 2001b, p.1)

The *Home Comments Sheet* (p.30) is a questionnaire that asks parents for their views on how their child relates to others and makes friends outside of the school, nursery or playgroup environment. There is a section on parents' priorities for developing their child's social play and a question asking what information they would like. Parents have a major role as partners in collecting and reviewing assessment information and in planning and delivering intervention (DfES, 2001a; DfES/DoH, 2004). The literature on social play emphasises the importance of obtaining information about opportunities, experiences and skills at home and in the wider community, in addition to school settings, in order to plan meaningful interventions (Mesibov, Adams and Klinger, 1997; Overton and Rausch, 2002). Information from parents is an essential part of assessment for children with autistic spectrum disorders because of the variability of the children's behaviours. Differences between home and school-based profiles contribute to a better understanding of the children's functioning, giving a more accurate assessment (Hart, 1995; Howlin, 1998; Tassé and Lecavalier, 2000).

Play Observation Sheets

> A systematic approach to direct observation is recommended to examine communication, social interaction and play skills. (Le Couteur, 2003, p.35)

Social play is not amenable to formal testing. Instead, systematic observational assessment in natural settings is recommended. Observation lends itself to different settings. This flexibility is helpful when assessing social play in children with autistic spectrum disorders (ASDs) because different situations affect the frequency and presence/absence of play behaviours (Howlin, 1998). Observing over time is useful for capturing infrequently occurring but significant events, such as emerging skills and the influence of structure, prompting and play partners (Wolfberg and Schuler, 1999).

How to use the Play Observation Sheets

1. Entries on the *Play Observation Sheets* come from two sources of information: direct observation and knowledge of the child. Combining these sources is considered to be the most reliable approach to qualitative assessment (Tilstone 1998).

2. The *Play Observation Sheets* are divided into six types of play:

    *   Early Social Play (reaction to others and reciprocal i.e. two-way play, p.32)

    *   Unoccupied (no purposeful activity apparent, p.33)

    *   Independent Play (diversity of the child's own play, p.34)

    *   Peer Play (extent of social participation, play preferences and social strategies, pp.35–37)

    *   Advanced Group Play (more sophisticated group and team skills, p.38)

    *   Friendship Skills (understanding, forming and maintaining friendships, p.39).

    At the beginning of each type of play is a key elements description outlining the main focus.

3. Examine all six types of play before using the *Play Observation Sheets*. More than one section will be relevant because a child at any developmental stage will show different types of play behaviour at different times. The development path for children with autistic spectrum disorders is usually atypical.

4. Each *Play Observation Sheet* has three main sections:

    *   *Key Social Play Markers*: the skills which mark the development of that type of social play. Markers include behaviours, levels and strategies, and are subdivided into small-steps component skills.

    *   *Assessment Rating*: for recording frequency of occurrence, prompting and areas that need working on. It identifies 'emerging' skills with potential for intervention. As the SPR is a skills-based assessment, no entry is made for skills that have not developed or have not been observed.

    *   *Comments*: for describing the context and how this affects the child.

    The 'Peer Play' section has two additional sheets for recording play preferences and social play strategies.

5. Enter observations, knowledge of the child and parents' views onto the *Play Observation Sheets*. Date the entries. The format of the *Play Observation Sheets* encourages you to analyse the information as it is entered.

6. For items that need addressing, tick the *Needs to work on* column when entries are made. This makes it easier to identify areas for intervention when looking back at the assessment data. The exception is the 'Unoccupied' section, which mainly describes behaviours that practitioners and carers will want to reduce. Although periods of being unoccupied form a normal part of play, it is the extent to which children with ASDs appear unoccupied that often causes concern.

7. It is important to record the child in various activities, across settings and with different play partners so as to identify which behaviours are one-offs, peer dependent or context bound. Less structured times like playtime, lunchtime and transition between activities often provide the best opportunities for observing social play. Remember that the purpose is not to assess *elicited* social interaction such as during formal lessons.

8. As far as possible make the observation part of routine practice so that it is unobtrusive. Observers should respect the child's privacy and dignity at all times. The child's response to being observed should also be monitored. Observation must stop if the child shows anxiety or reacts adversely.

Practitioner Rating of Peer Relationships

The *Practitioner Rating of Peer Relationships* (p.40) gives an overview of the child's response to peers and their reaction to him or her. Both perspectives are important because of the reciprocal nature of social play (Hepler, 1997; Howes, 1987). The *Practitioner Rating* has a graded scale, a friendship component and an 'opposites' scale which describes important dimensions of peer relationships that are difficult to capture using observation alone. The *Practitioner Rating* adds a further perspective, a means of checking adult assumptions against preferences expressed by the children themselves, and child preferences against practitioner observation of actual interaction. Updating the sheet will indicate whether progress is being made. It is worth noting that reliability and validity studies have concluded that practitioner ratings are a useful adjunct to observed behaviours and sociometric assessment but are not viable as a sole measure of social play.

How to use the Practitioner Rating

The first part of the *Practitioner Rating* ('Child's response to peers') uses a graded rating scale along a continuum. Tick the descriptions that correspond to the child's response to his or her peers and to the presence or absence of friendships.

The second part of the *Practitioner Rating* ('Peers' response to child') examines peers' attitudes, with a description based on three opposite dimensions. For each of the three dimensions, place a cross on a point on the line that corresponds to peers' attitudes to the child.

Compare findings on the *Practitioner Rating* with those from the *Peer Preferences Chart* (p.41) and the *Questionnaire about Friends* (pp.42–43) to determine whether intervention is required and which aspects to address.

Peer Preferences Chart

Social skills are not the only factors that affect peer relationships. Social competence depends as much on the perception and reaction of peers as on the development of individual skills (DiSalvo and Oswald, 2002; Hepler, 1997). Peers play a critical role in developing social competence, serving a variety of functions such as emotional support to face new or difficult situations and peer tutoring, facilitating forms of play. Children's status (acceptance/rejection by peers) is crucial. Early social experiences have been found to affect interpersonal relationships in adolescence and adulthood. Links have also been found between positive and negative peer rating and later mental health status (see Appendix 4).

The *Peer Preferences Chart* (p.41) examines status, attitudes and perceptions. Its purpose is to identify:

- the extent to which children are accepted/rejected by peers

- the extent to which children have friends

- children who are socially isolated or have difficulty relating to peers

- ways to improve attitudes and relationships within a child's peer group.

The *Peer Preferences Chart* is based on sociometry: a technique for measuring popularity, reciprocal friendships and social participation. It provides information from the children's perspective on how peers are viewed by others, that is, their sociometric status (see studies by Asher and Hymel, 1981; Frederickson and Furnham, 2001). Sociometry is a relatively simple way to assess social relationships in play situations and can be integrated into class activity, as explained below.

Important considerations

Before using the *Peer Preferences Chart*, practitioners should be aware of several important ethical considerations. The chart should only be used one at a time with children who are familiar with each other, for example children in the same class or regular activity group. It is important to protect the identity of the children and the confidentiality of their choices. This may be achieved by keeping the activity within school, using photographs from the school database and ensuring records are securely filed. By heightening their awareness, children may begin to view certain peers more negatively than they already do. Sensitivity is required to avoid compounding the social exclusion or isolation of negatively rated children. The process may be seen to sanction negative comments and this will need to be monitored. Repeating the activity is recommended to check reliability of ratings.

Materials required

- A digital or Polaroid camera (for in-house processing to protect children's identity).

- Individual photographs of each child in the class or group being assessed.

- A group photo of the children being assessed. This may be a small group, a whole class or more than one class, depending on the breadth of peer relationships being examined.

- Five photographs of food for the pre-training task explained below.

- Three boxes for posting the photographs. On the front of each, paste one of these face symbols plus text:

  ☺ I like a lot. ☺ I like a bit. ☹ I don't like.

- One container labelled with two happy face symbols and text:

  ☺ ☺ I like the most.

- The *Peer Preferences Chart* to enter children's choices.

What to do

1. Materials are presented visually to one child at a time, using photographs, face symbols and text. The text is adapted from studies by Asher *et al.* (1979) and Guralnick *et al.* (1996). To check the children's understanding of the rating procedure, each child is given the pre-training task using the five food photographs. Children are individually asked to assign each photo to one of the three boxes, according to how much he or she likes that food.

2. If the pre-training task is understood, the children are individually shown photographs of each child in the peer group. The photographs are presented singly and the child is asked: 'How much do you like to play with this person?' The child assigns each photo to one of the three boxes. These ratings are entered on the chart, by ticking the relevant box next to the name of the peer.

3. All the photographs posted in the ☺ box are presented again to the child. He or she is asked 'Who do you like to play with the most?'. The child places the most liked photo/s in the container with the two happy face symbols to denote his or her 'best friend'. Place a check mark in the *Best Friend* column for nominated peers.

4. The containers are removed and the child is shown a photo of the whole group or class. He or she is asked: 'Who do you play with most days?' Enter responses in the *Everyday Playmate* column.

Scoring the Peer Preferences Chart

For the *play with* rating: ☺ scores 3; ☺ scores 2; ☹ scores 1. Add these scores together to give the *total rating* each child receives from the group. The average measure of overall acceptance/likeability for each child may then be calculated using the 'Outcome of Peer Evaluation' sheet. So, for example, if a child receives a rating of ☺ from three peers, he or she would score nine in the *A lot* column (and so on). The average likeability of each child can be worked out by dividing the total rating score by three. Every score for *likes to play with a lot* and *likes to play with a bit* counts as a positive nomination. Every score for *does not like to play with* counts as a negative nomination. You can also add, in the final column, the number of *best friend* ratings each child receives.

The positive and negative ratings indicate degrees of acceptance or rejection by peers, identifying children at risk in peer relationships. Low-status children are identified by a low acceptance/likeability score (few ☺ and ☺ ratings), high negative nominations (many ☹ ratings), no best friend nomination and being least chosen as an Everyday Playmate. The *best friend* column shows most preferred playmates. Comparing the children's nominations will identify mutual friends. This information may also be checked against the *Practitioner Rating* and the *Questionnaire about Friends*. The *Everyday Playmate* nomination on the *Peer Preferences Chart* allows practitioners and carers to check actual playmates against expressed preferences. This information helps to identify children who give or receive negative attention, for example those who are manipulated, bullied or develop an obsessional interest in others. The *Comments* section on the *Peer Preferences Chart* is for recording qualitative information, such as the children's understanding of the task, any comments they make and the reason for their choices.

Questionnaire about Friends

The *Questionnaire about Friends* (pp.42–43) explores the children's view of friendship. It evaluates their concept of and interest in friends, identifies similar interests that might form the basis of a friendship, and indicates budding friendships that could be supported. The *Questionnaire about Friends* provides a means for self-assessment. Involving children in the process of assessment is considered pivotal to accurate evaluation and to the development of self-awareness through the identification of skills, needs and progress (DfES, 2001a; Harrison, 1998; Jordan and Powell, 1995; Lewis, 1996).

The *Questionnaire about Friends* should be filled in by the children. It includes questions around practical activities at school and likes or dislikes. Graphics illustrate the concept of independent/paired/group activity and help pupils to self-record. Responses indicate the level at which children tolerate being with peers and the basis for their friendship choices (for example, familiarity, proximity, likes or dislikes, help received, skills, interests, sociability, personality). Comparing baseline (first) assessment with subsequent questionnaires measures progress in the children's understanding and attitudes. Determining children's understanding of friendship is crucial to deciding the level and content of intervention (Attwood, 1998; Bauminger, Shulman and Agam 2003). This is particularly important for children who receive a low evaluation on the *Peer Preferences Chart* and the *Practitioner Rating*.

How to use the Questionnaire about Friends

1. The questionnaire should be completed individually, if possible as an independent task. Children should express their own ideas. If working with a group of children, ensure that answers are not copied.

2. Introduce the questionnaire by explaining its purpose – to write about *friends*.

3. Go through the questions to check that the child understands the text and the graphics.

4. If a child struggles to understand the questions, offer an alternative task on friendship, such as working on a picture that depicts friends or listening to a story about friends.

5. If a child understands the questions but struggles to write answers, offer to act as scribe.

6. Compare the child's answers with information from the *Peer Preferences Chart* and *Practitioner Rating*. If intervention is indicated, use the Friendship Skills section in Chapter 4 (p.66) and the Small Steps chart (Appendix 3) to identify specific targets.

Scoring the SPR Assessment

Scoring the Social Play Record is optional. The scoring system is a tally of social play behaviours that are rated according to frequency of occurrence and the need for prompting. Items have not been weighted for other reasons, such as comparative difficulty. Development of the Social Play Record is an ongoing process, and user feedback on this prototype scoring system and on the instructions for using it would be welcome (a photocopiable evaluation form for this purpose can be found on p.138). Despite its simplicity, the scoring system provides:

- summative information, giving a summary of achievement in each area of social play at any given point in time, allowing comparisons to be made and progress to be monitored

- diagnostic information, identifying gaps and areas of little or no progress

- cumulative information, as items are developmentally ordered.

How to score the Social Play Record

The Social Play Record has a maximum score of 180 points. This is a combined score, obtained by adding the scores from the different assessment measures.

SCORING THE PLAY OSBSERVATION SHEETS

The maximum score on the *Play Observation Sheets* is 159. Use *Scores for the Play Observation Sheets* (p.47). The different types of social play are listed in the first box. The key social play markers are given in the boxes running across each row. There is one box for each key marker described on the *Play Observation Sheets*. The letters in the top left-hand corner of the boxes correspond to the items under each type of social play. For example, 'Early Social Play (Reactive)' box A is for entering the score for item A ('Responds to people') on the Assessment. Items are rated for frequency of occurrence and whether prompting is required: often scores 3; sometimes scores 2; prompted scores 1; needs to work on scores 0. Some items are further subdivided, for example 'Independent Play' box D. The subdivisions in box D refer to the five key behaviours listed under 'Imaginative play': for example, box D, subdivision 3 refers to item 3 ('Pretends one object is another').

The totals for each type of social play are entered in the right-hand boxes under *Social Play Scores*. The total score for all the items on the *Play Observation Sheets* is entered in the bottom right-hand box under *Total Score*. The maximum score, if all items are rated as occurring often, is 159. Six items are excluded from the scoring: the five items in the 'Unoccupied' section and the 'Preoccupied' item in the 'Independent Play' section. Although these behaviours are seen in routinely developing children, practitioners may wish to discourage children with social interaction needs from spending too much time in unoccupied or preoccupied activity to the exclusion of more social types of play.

SCORING THE PRACTITIONER RATING OF PEER RELATIONSHIPS

Use the 'Score for Practitioner Rating of Peer Relationships' boxes. The maximum score is 8.

- 'Child's response to peers' (maximum score 5): Entries under 'Solitary' and 'Hesitant' do not score. For entries under 'Active': often scores 3; sometimes scores 2; prompted scores 1; rarely or never scores 0. For 'Friendships', score 0 if the child has no mutal (i.e. reciprocal) friends; score 1 if the child has one mutual friend; score 2 if the child has more than one mutual friend.

- 'Peers' response to child' (maximum score 3): Peers *accept* more than 50 per cent of the time scores 1. Peers *acknowledge* more than 50 per cent of the time scores 1. Peers *support* more than 50 per cent of the time scores 1.

SCORING THE PEER PREFERENCES CHART

Use the 'Score for the Peer Preferences Chart' boxes. The maximum score is 3. Receives more nominations on *likes to play with* than *does not like to play with* scores 1. Receives no nominations on *does not like to play with* scores 1. Receives a mutual *best friend* rating scores 1. Mutual best friends nominate each other as 'I like the most'.

SCORING THE QUESTIONNAIRE ABOUT FRIENDS

Use the 'Score for the Questionnaire about Friends' boxes. The maximum score is 10. The scoring is as follows:

- *In class I like to work…* This is a lead-in question so is not scored.

- *In PE I choose…* If child independently chooses a partner for PE or other activity, score 1.

- *At playtime or break I like to be…* If the child prefers to be with others score 1.

- *I like to play…* If the answer includes social games score 1.

- *I don't like to play…* If the answer does not include social games score 1.

- *I feel happy when people…* If the answer involves social interaction score 1 (e.g. share toys/play with me/like me/are friends).

- *I feel sad when people…* If the answer involves social interaction score 1 (e.g. pick on me/hurt me/won't be friends/argue).

- *A friend is someone who…* For one appropriate concept score 1; for two or more appropriate concepts score 2. If the answer specifies what the child can do for a friend score 3.

- *My friends are…* If the child names one mutual friend score 1.

THE HOME COMMENTS SHEET

There is no scoring system for the *Home Comments Sheet* because the information is purely qualitative.

THE PROFILE OF SCORES

For a see-at-a-glance summary, enter scores from each assessment measure onto the *Profile of Scores Sheet* (p.50).

THE PROGRESS CHART

A child's total score on the Social Play Record Assessment may be plotted on the *Progress Chart* (p.51) in the form of a bar or line graph. This provides a see-at-a-glance quantitative summary of the assessment findings at any point in time. Entering total scores from subsequent assessments shows whether progress is being made overall. An example is given in Appendix 1. To obtain a profile of skills, needs and progress, compare scores across the assessment measures of the Social Play Record (pp.47–49).

Planning Intervention

The Social Play Record provides a means to share knowledge in a structured way that is useful for assessing skills and needs and guiding intervention. Its purpose is to generate recommendations for intervention. Part 2, *Links to Intervention*, relates assessment findings to approaches, strategies, activities and resources for each stage of social play. The sections in *Links to Intervention* correspond to those in the Social Play Record Assessment.

Use the assessment information to identify established skills (often present), emerging skills (sometimes present or used when prompted), and absent skills (not observed). The Assessment rating, and particularly the *Needs to work on* column on the *Play Observation Sheets* (pp.32–39), completed as information on social play is entered, will guide the choice of intervention targets. Aim for targets that are likely to bring early success. Emerging skills are usually easier to develop than absent ones. However, some skills, particularly joint attention, are more critical and fundamental than others and should be addressed first. Refer to the *Links to Intervention* section for guidance.

Choose three targets to enter on the *Planning Sheet* (p.46). More than three becomes unworkable. The choice will be based on practitioners' and parents' knowledge of the child's needs and priorities, but as the Social Play Record follows a broadly developmental sequence the earlier levels are likely to be easier. Use strengths (established and emerging skills) to minimise the effect of difficulties. Enter the three targets on the *Planning Sheet*, one in each of the three numbered boxes. Below each numbered target is a space to record the outcome of intervention, prior to the child's next review (a completed example is given in Appendix 1, p.82).

The Social Play Record's specific, skills-based focus and small-steps structure make it easy to produce child-friendly Independent Education Plan (IEP) targets. These could be shown in written and/or pictorial format, for example using *Writing with Symbols* (Widgit Software, 2000) as shown in Appendix 1 (p.88). The SPR is designed to be used as an ongoing record, with new information entered as it is gained. Alternatively, it can be updated at intervals to fit in with target setting for individual education, therapy or care plans and the review process.

Sharing information and decision making often leads to better outcomes (DfES/DoH 2002, 2004). Following completion, the Social Play Record Assessment and proposed intervention targets should be discussed by parents, practitioners and, where appropriate, the child. Family concerns and priorities should be addressed and goals and strategies negotiated. Home–school collaboration encourages consistency of approach and supports skill maintenance and generalisation (Wood, 1995).

3

The SPR Asessment Sheets

Social Play Record Assessment

HOME COMMENTS SHEET

The Social Play Record looks at how children play, relate to others and make friends. Its purpose is to find ways to help the children improve their play and social communication skills. This *Home Comments Sheet* is for you to provide information about how your child plays and relates to others outside of school. There is a question about your priorities for developing his or her social play and a section asking what information you would like.

Child's name: Date:

Sheet completed by:

At home

How does your child occupy his or her free time?

What does he or she respond to? What does he or she do most often? What does he or she enjoy? Does he or she have any favourite objects, toys or games? Does he or she have any special interests or hobbies? What is he or she good at?

With whom does your child play?

Family? Friends? Visitors? Alone? Who gets the most from him or her?

How does your child play with others?

Does he or she start the play or wait for others? Does he or she copy others? Share? Take turns?

Social Play Record Assessment

HOME COMMENTS SHEET

Outside the home

(for example: playgrounds, activity centres, clubs, parties)

What opportunities does your child have to socialise with others?

What is he or she like with other children?

What are other children like with him or her?

Do you have any concerns about his or her social play? If yes, please explain.

Priorities for developing my child's social play should be:

Information for parents/carers

Areas I would like to discuss:

Areas I would like more information on:

I would like to learn ways to improve my child's social play skills.   **Yes / No**

Social Play Record Assessment

EARLY SOCIAL PLAY

Reactive play

Key elements: Child reacts to adults who impinge on his or her space.

Name: Date:

KEY SOCIAL PLAY MARKERS	ASSESSMENT RATING				COMMENTS
	Often	Sometimes	When prompted	Needs to work on	Describe context and how it affects child (e.g. play partners, activities, prompts)
A. Responds to people.	☐	☐	☐	☐	
B. Responds to own name.	☐	☐	☐	☐	
C. Looks at/accepts objects offered.	☐	☐	☐	☐	
D. Enjoys social games (e.g. tickles; peek-a-boo; chase)	☐	☐	☐	☐	

Reciprocal play

Key elements: Child takes a more active part in the play. Joint activity, imitation, turn-taking begins.

Name: Date:

KEY SOCIAL PLAY MARKERS	ASSESSMENT RATING				COMMENTS
	Often	Sometimes	When prompted	Needs to work on	Describe context and how it affects child (e.g. play partners, activities, prompts)
A. Copies facial expression and gestures (e.g. waves goodbye).	☐	☐	☐	☐	
B. Shows: points or brings objects to show.	☐	☐	☐	☐	
C. Shares: offers/shares objects (e.g. food, books).	☐	☐	☐	☐	
D. Actively joins in partner games (e.g. action rhymes, ball games).	☐	☐	☐	☐	

Social Play Record Assessment

UNOCCUPIED

Key elements: No purposeful activity apparent.

Name: Date:

OBSERVATIONS	ASSESSMENT RATING			COMMENTS
	Often	Sometimes	Rarely or never	Describe context and how it affects child
A. Sits in one spot or stands around.	☐	☐	☐	
B. Wanders aimlessly or walks the perimeter.	☐	☐	☐	
C. Fleetingly watches anything of momentary interest.	☐	☐	☐	
D. Seems unaware of the presence of others.	☐	☐	☐	
E. Blocks others out or resists others' attempts to join in, e.g. puts fingers in ears, closes eyes, hums, vocalises, screams, turns or moves away.	☐	☐	☐	

Social Play Record Assessment

INDEPENDENT PLAY

Key elements: Plays alone and independently with toys different from those used by children within speaking distance. Pursues own activity without reference to others.

Name: Date:

KEY COGNITIVE LEVELS	ASSESSMENT RATING				COMMENTS
	Often	Sometimes	When prompted	Needs to work on	Desribe context and how it affects child (e.g. situation, materials, activities, prompts)
A. Sensorimotor play Uses senses appropriately to explore objects.	☐	☐	☐	☐	
B. Functional play Uses toys or materials according to their intended function.	☐	☐	☐	☐	
C. Constructional play Uses materials (e.g. bricks, Lego, Duplo) to construct something.	☐	☐	☐	☐	
D. Imaginative play 1. Pretends actions or feelings.	☐	☐	☐	☐	
2. Uses imaginary objects in play.	☐	☐	☐	☐	
3. Pretends one object is another.	☐	☐	☐	☐	
4. Pretend play follows a sequence.	☐	☐	☐	☐	
5. Engages in role play.	☐	☐	☐	☐	
E. Preoccupied play For example, with body movements, senses, actions, specific objects or parts of objects, activities or interests.	☐	☐	☐	☐	

Social Play Record Assessment

PEER PLAY

Extent of social participation

Key elements: As described in boxes below.

Name: Date:

TYPE OF PEER PLAY AND KEY MARKERS	ASSESSMENT RATING				COMMENTS
	Often	Sometimes	When prompted	Needs to work on	Describe context and how it affects child
OBSERVER					
A. Watches peers from within speaking distance.	☐	☐	☐	☐	
B. Comments on peers' activity.	☐	☐	☐	☐	
C. Turns towards peers.	☐	☐	☐	☐	
PARALLEL					
A. Plays alongside peers but independently.	☐	☐	☐	☐	
B. Copies peers.	☐	☐	☐	☐	
C. Looks and smiles at those he or she is copying.	☐	☐	☐	☐	
ASSOCIATIVE					
A. Responds positively to peers' approaches.	☐	☐	☐	☐	
B. Exchanges or shares materials.	☐	☐	☐	☐	
C. Speaks to peers.	☐	☐	☐	☐	
CO-OPERATIVE					
A. Shares materials and activities or goals, taking turns.	☐	☐	☐	☐	
B. Offers suggestions for attaining goals or for extending play themes.	☐	☐	☐	☐	
C. Complements and exchanges roles.	☐	☐	☐	☐	

PEER PLAY

Play preferences

Name: Date:

MATERIALS, TOYS OR ACTIVITIES	PEERS	CONTEXTS (THEMES AND SETTINGS)

Social Play Record Assessment

PEER PLAY

Social Play tasks and strategies

Name: Date:

Describe social play *strategies* the child uses and rate their frequency.
Scores: often = 3; sometimes = 2; when prompted = 1; rarely or never = 0

SOCIAL PLAY TASKS	APPROPRIATE AND EFFECTIVE STRATEGIES	INAPPROPRIATE OR INEFFECTIVE STRATEGIES	NEEDS TO WORK ON
A. Entering peer play			
B. Maintaining peer play			
C. Resolving peer conflict			
D. Exiting peer play			
E. Avoiding peer play			

Social Play Record Assessment

ADVANCED GROUP PLAY

Key elements: More sophisticated group skills emerge, such as group identity and roles; use of compromise, negotiation and persuasion; competition.

Name: Date:

KEY SOCIAL PLAY MARKERS	ASSESSMENT RATING				COMMENTS
	Often	**Sometimes**	**When prompted**	**Needs to work on**	Describe context and how it affects child (e.g. situation, peers, activities, prompts)
A. Identifies with a peer group.	☐	☐	☐	☐	
B. Conforms to group norms (activities/attitudes/ dress/speech).	☐	☐	☐	☐	
C. Applies rules flexibly.	☐	☐	☐	☐	
D. Uses strategies for compromise, negotiation, persuasion and reconciliation.	☐	☐	☐	☐	
E. Copes with competition, winning and losing.	☐	☐	☐	☐	
F. Participates as a team player.	☐	☐	☐	☐	

Social Play Record Assessment

FRIENDSHIP SKILLS

Key elements: Acceptance and rejection of and by peers. Understanding of 'friendship' develops. Formation and maintenance of relationships.

Name: Date:

KEY SOCIAL PLAY MARKERS	ASSESSMENT RATING				COMMENTS
	Often	Sometimes	When prompted	Needs to work on	Describe context and how it affects child (e.g. situation, peers, activities, prompts)
A. Making friends					
1. Peers accept and choose child.	☐	☐	☐	☐	
2. Child interacts with peers in preference to adults.	☐	☐	☐	☐	
3. Child has mutual friendships (i.e. laughs and smiles with friends; spends 30% time or more with; friendships lasts over time).	☐	☐	☐	☐	
B. Interactional style					
1. Style is appropriate to peer group.	☐	☐	☐	☐	
C. Conversational skills					
1. Inititates conversation with peers.	☐	☐	☐	☐	
2. Listens and responds to peers.	☐	☐	☐	☐	
3. Talks with, not at peers, taking conversational turns.	☐	☐	☐	☐	
4. Ends conversation appropriately.	☐	☐	☐	☐	
D. Sustaining friendships					
1. Shows concern for friend's feelings.	☐	☐	☐	☐	
2. Shares own interests and activities.	☐	☐	☐	☐	
3. Seeks solutions to avoid or resolve conflict.	☐	☐	☐	☐	
4. Accommodates friend's preferences, interests, needs.	☐	☐	☐	☐	
5. Offers and seeks practical support; e.g. lends/shares items, helps, advises, defends.	☐	☐	☐	☐	
6. Shares experiences, feelings, secrets, humour.	☐	☐	☐	☐	

Social Play Record Assessment

PRACTITIONER RATING OF PEER RELATIONSHIPS

Name: Date:

A. CHILD'S RESPONSE TO PEERS:

Tick box as appropriate

SOLITARY: Child is disinterested/withdrawn/actively avoids contact with peers.

☐ Never or rarely   ☐ Sometimes   ☐ Often

HESITANT: Child is shy/socially immature (inept entry skills; fumbled attempts).

☐ Never or rarely   ☐ Sometimes   ☐ Often

ACTIVE: Child is sociable.

☐ Never or rarely   ☐ Prompted   ☐ Sometimes   ☐ Often

FRIENDSHIPS:

☐ Child has no mutual friends.

☐ Child has one mutual friend.

☐ Child has more than one mutual friend.

B. PEERS' RESPONSE TO CHILD

A completed example is shown in Appendix I.

Reject	50%	Accept
Isolate		Invite to join
Actively avoid		Offer toys or materials
Show hostility		Assign roles or tasks
Mock or bully		
Ignore		**Acknowledge**
Indifferent		Smile
Disinterested		Greet or speak to
Tolerate		**Support**
Accept presence		Adapt speech/behaviour
Offer low-status role		Take responsibility for
Over-protect		Show or guide

Social Play Record Assessment

PEER PREFERENCES CHART

Name: Date:

NAMES OF CHILDREN IN PEER GROUP*	LIKES TO PLAY WITH A LOT ☺	LIKES TO PLAY WITH A BIT ☺	DOES NOT LIKE TO PLAY WITH ☹	BEST FRIEND** ☺☺	EVERYDAY PLAYMATES ***
1.					
2.					
3.					
4.					
5.					
6.					
7.					
8.					
9.					
10.					

* Present photos individually to one child at a time. Ask: 'How much do you like to play with this person?'

** Re-present the ☺ photos. Ask: 'Who do you like to play with the most?' Place a check mark against nominated peers.

*** Present a photo of the whole group or class. Ask: 'Who do you play with most days?'

Comments:

Social Play Record Assessment

QUESTIONNAIRE ABOUT FRIENDS

Name: _____

Class: _____

Date: _____

Circle your choice and fill in the gaps

In class I like to work:

by myself

with another person

in a group

In PE I choose _____ **to be my partner.**

At playtime or break I like to be:

by myself

with a friend

with a group of friends

♡

I like to play _____

⦸ (heart with line through it)

I don't like to play _____

☺

I feel happy when people _____

☹

I feel sad when people _____

A friend is someone who _____

My friends are _____

Social Play Record Assessment

SUMMARY SHEET

Name: Date:

	Often	Sometimes	When prompted	Rarely or never

TYPE OF PLAY

Early Social Play (Reactive)

Child reacts to adult who impinges on his or her space.   □ □ □ □

Early Social Play (Reciprocal)

Child takes more active part in the play. Joint activity, beginnings of imitation and turn-taking.   □ □ □ □

Unoccupied

No purposeful activity apparent.   □ □ □ □

Independent Play

Plays alone and independently with toys different from those used by children within speaking distance. Pursues own activity without reference to others. Makes no effort to get close to other children.   □ □ □ □

Observer

Child is a spectator. Passive observation without actual participation.   □ □ □ □

Parallel Play

Child plays *beside* rather than with others, within the same physical space but independently.   □ □ □ □

Child plays with toys/materials similar to those around him or her and *imitates* others, but maintains independent play.   □ □ □ □

Associative Play

Plays *with* other children, sharing materials, but play is still independent, with each child playing as he or she wishes. The activity may be similar or identical but is not organised around any *mutual* activity or goal. Awareness of others develops.   □ □ □ □

Co-operative and Co-ordinated Play

Play is co-ordinated with and complements others' play. Sharing of attention, materials, activities. Common goals and complementary roles.   □ □ □ □

Advanced Group Play

More sophisticated group skills emerge, such as group identity and roles; uses compromise, negotiation and persuasion; coping with competition.   □ □ □ □

Friendship Skills

Acceptance and rejection of and by peers. Understanding of 'friendship' develops. Formation and maintenance of friendships.   □ □ □ □

Social Play Record Assessment

CLASS SUMMARY PROFILE

Class: _____   Date: _____

Type of Social Play Tick or date boxes	Names of pupils										
Early Social Play (Reactive)											
Early social Play (Reciprocal)											
Unoccupied											
Independent Play											
Observer											
Parallel Play											
Associative Play											
Co-operative Play											
Advanced Group Play											
Friendship Skills											

Social Play Record Assessment

PLANNING SHEET

Name: Date:

INTERVENTION TARGETS FOR SOCIAL PLAY

Target 1:

Outcome:

Target 2:

Outcome:

Target 3:

Outcome:

Social Play Record Assessment

SCORE FOR THE PLAY OBSERVATION SHEETS

Name: Date:

TYPES OF SOCIAL PLAY	KEY SOCIAL PLAY MARKERS (Item letters are in top left corner of boxes) Scores: often = 3; sometimes = 2; when prompted = 1; rarely or never = 0					Social play score
Early social play (Reactive)	A ‾3	B ‾3	C ‾3	D ‾3		‾12
Early social play (Reciprocal)	A ‾3	B ‾3	C ‾3	D ‾3		‾12
Independent play	A ‾3	B ‾3	C ‾3	D ‾15		‾24
Peer play: Observer	A ‾3	B ‾3	C ‾3			‾9
Peer play: Parallel	A ‾3	B ‾3	C ‾3			‾9
Peer play: Associative	A ‾3	B ‾3	C ‾3			‾9
Peer play: Co-operative	A ‾3	B ‾3	C ‾3			‾9
Peer play: Strategies	A ‾3	B ‾3	C ‾3	D ‾3	E ‾3	‾15
Advanced group	A ‾3	B ‾3	C ‾3	D ‾3	E ‾3	F ‾3 ‾18
Friendship skills	A ‾9	B ‾3	C ‾12	D ‾18		‾42
					Total score	‾159

SCORES FOR THE PRACTITIONER RATING AND PEER PREFERENCES CHART

Name: Date:

Score for Practitioner Rating of Peer Relationships

Criteria for scoring	Score
A: Child's response to peers ACTIVE: score 0 for rarely or never; score 1 for prompted; score 2 for sometimes; score 3 for often. Entries under 'Solitary' and 'Hesitant' do not score. FRIENDSHIPS: score 0 if the child has no mutual friends; score 1 if child has one mutual friend; score 2 if child has more than one mutual friend.	5̄
B: Peers' response to child • Peers accept more than 50% of the time scores 1. • Peers acknowledge more than 50% of the time scores 1. • Peers support more than 50% of the times scores 1.	3̄
Total score	8̄

Score for Peer Preferences Chart

Criteria for scoring	Score
Receives more nominations on *likes to play with* than *does not like to play with*.	1̄
Receives no nomination on *does not like to play with*.	1̄
Receives a mutual *best friend* nomination.	1̄
Total score	3̄

Social Play Record Assessment

SCORE FOR THE QUESTIONNAIRE ABOUT FRIENDS

Name: Date:

Score for Questionnaire about Friends

Items on the Questionnaire	Criteria for scoring	Score
In PE I choose…	Independently chooses a partner for PE or other activity.	‾1
At playtime or break I like to be …	Circles *with a friend* or *with a group of friends*.	‾1
I like to play…	Answer includes social games, i.e. games with others.	‾1
I do not like to play…	Answer does not include social games.	‾1
I feel happy when people…	Answer refers to social interaction.	‾1
I feel sad when people…	Answer refers to social interaction.	‾1
A friend is someone who…	One concept of friendship (e.g. plays with me) scores 1. Two or more concepts (e.g. shares things; helps you) scores 2. Answer includes what the child can do for a friend scores 3.	‾3
My friends are…	Names a *mutual* friend.	‾1
	Total score	‾10

Social Play Record Assessment

PROFILE OF SCORES

Name: Date:

Assessment Measure	Score
Play Observation sheets	159
Practitioner Rating of Peer Relationships	8
Peer Preferences Chart	3
Questionnaire about Friends	10
Total score on the Social Play Record	180

A child's total score on the Social Play Record Assessment may be entered on the Progress Chart in the form of a bar chart or a line graph. An example is given in Appendix 1.

Social Play Record Assessment

PROGRESS CHART

Name:

SPR SCORE																		
180	170	160	150	140	130	120	110	100	90	80	70	60	50	40	30	20	10	0

ASSESSMENT DATES

PART 2

LINKS TO INTERVENTION

4

How it all Fits Together

There is a growing body of research which shows that structured intervention based on functional assessment leads to gains in social play (see Appendix 4). Assessment is the first step in identifying skills and needs and choosing appropriate intervention targets. Assessment is explained in Part 1, *User Guide for the SPR Assessment*. Part 2 looks at *Links to Intervention*. Its purpose is to relate findings on the SPR Assessment to approaches, strategies, activities and resources. There are numerous interventions and methods for developing social play (Jordan, 2003; McConnell, 2002; Terpstra, Higgins and Pierce, 2002). The most effective include tried and tested strategies: for example, visual presentation, structured format, building on strengths, interests and self-esteem, and developing social support networks. But knowing when and how to use which approach can be confusing. *Links to Intervention* offers step-by-step guidance on choosing approaches and resources for each type of social play. Intervention is tailored to the individual child's needs from his or her point of entry on the SPR and is adapted over time to reflect maturation, skill development and changes in circumstances.

The SPR Assessment identifies the type(s) of social play in which a child usually engages without support and the level at which skills sometimes appear – in other words, the child's established skills and emerging skills. Intervention then focuses on developing emerging skills rather than concentrating on deficits. Targets chosen to stabilise emerging skills are often easiest for a child to learn. Targets are entered on the *Planning Sheet* (p.46). The sections in *Links to Intervention* correspond to those in the SPR Assessment. Sections refer to the different types of social play: early social play, unoccupied or preoccupied, independent play, peer play, advanced group play and friendship skills. Within each section are suggestions and resources for how to work on or from that stage of social play. Breaking down skills into small steps helps to plan the transition from one stage to the next, clarifying what to work on and when. Small Steps guidance is provided in Appendix 3, based on the development of play in neurotypical children and in children with autistic spectrum disorders. Practitioners will also need to teach children when and how to use each step appropriately, that is, the social understanding that underpins the skill.

The Small Steps section is comprehensive in order to cover the developmental range from early infancy to adolescence. However, it is not necessary to work on all the small steps listed under each type of social play. Choose the most relevant for the child and his or her situation. For example, a child may need to work on 'entry strategies' for peer play. The Small Steps chart for peer play entry skills (p.116) identifies several entry strategies, from which individual targets may be selected. Suggestions for developing this particular skill will be found in the 'Peer Play' section of this chapter.

Remember that social play develops over the long term. The Social Play Record is designed to address this. It is not practical or productive to try to work on everything at once or to focus solely on the child's difficulties. Work on areas that may be most successful (emerging skills) or beneficial to the child at that point in time (key skills). Work collaboratively, planning goals, sharing disappointments and celebrating achievements with colleagues, with the child and with his or her family.

It is also important to remember that social play is not a linear process, involving the acquisition of separate skills, but a transactional one. Social play develops through the interplay of multiple factors. All children, at whatever stage of social play, need a combination of *skill, opportunity* and *experience*: skill in knowing how to play, opportunities for social learning and experience in using skills and making the most of opportunities. Intervention that focuses solely on the skills/behaviours of the child with social interaction difficulties or teaches isolated skills out of context will be less than successful. Practitioners and parents need to acknowledge the significant effect of social and environmental influences and to adapt the social play environment to accommodate the children's differences and difficulties. Several interrelated strands of the work are usually undertaken simultaneously. For example, when developing entry skills, peers should be taught to recognise and respond to the overtures of the child with social interaction needs. Research has shown that when other children are taught to recognise, prompt and reinforce appropriate social behaviour, the rate and level of interaction improve (Appendix 4). The *Home Comments Sheet, Practitioner Rating* and *Peer Preferences* sections of the SPR Assessment look at peers' attitudes, behaviours and concerns. Taking this wider perspective helps to address issues of social inclusion.

Early Social Play

Early social play begins when a child *responds* to an adult's playful interaction. It develops into *reciprocal* interaction, with the child taking a more active part. The aims of early social play are:

- to increase awareness of others

- to develop understanding and use of *joint attention*. Joint attention is sharing the focus of attention with another person. It is fundamental to all social interaction and learning, particularly the development of communication, so this is a critical area for intervention.

- to develop playful social routines with a responsive adult
- to develop joint action routines within everyday situations.

Activities for developing joint attention, social routines and joint action routines are set out in the Small Steps 'Early Social Play' section (Appendix 3) and in Appendix 2, *Ideas and Templates for Developing Social Play*. The suggested resources outline numerous other ideas and activities.

Resources for children at the early social play stage

Aldred, C., Pollard, C., Phillips, R. and Adams, C. (2001) 'The Child's Talk Project: Multidisciplinary social communication intervention for children with autism and pervasive developmental disorder.' *Educational and Child Psychology 18*, 2, 76–87.

Cumine, V., Leach, J. and Stevenson, G. (2000) *Autism in the Early Years: A Practical Guide.* London: David Fulton Publishers.

Frost, L. and Bondy, A. (1994) *Picture Exchange Communication System Training Manual.* Cherry Hill, NJ: Pyramid Educational Consultants Inc (www.pecs.com).

Leicester County Council and Fosse Health Trust (1998) *Autism: How to Help your Young Child.* London: National Autistic Society Press.

Lynch, C. and Kidd, J. *Early Communication Skills.* Chesterfield: Winslow Press.

Moor, J. (2002) *Playing, Laughing and Learning with Children on the Autism Spectrum: A Practical Resource of Play Ideas for Parents and Carers.* London: Jessica Kingsley Publishers.

National Autistic Society *EarlyBird Programme* (www.nas.org.uk).

Newman, S. (1999) *Small Steps Forward.* London: Jessica Kingsley Publishers.

Nind, M. and Hewett, D. (1998) *Access to Communication.* London: David Fulton Publishers.

Play www.aristotle.net/theraplay/

Roberts, S. (2001) *Play Songs: Action Songs and Rhymes for Early Years.* London: A&C Black.

Potter, C. and Whittaker, C. (2001) *Enabling Communication in Children with Autism.* London: Jessica Kingsley Publishers. Chapter on proximal communication and minimal speech approach.

Prevezer, W. (2000) 'Musical Interaction and children with autism.' In S. Powell (ed.) *Helping Children with Autism to Learn.* London: David Fulton Publishers.

Sonders, S. (2002) *Giggle Time: Establishing the Social Connection.* London: Jessica Kingsley Publishers.

Sussman, F. (1999) *Hanen 'More Than Words' Parent Programme.* Toronto: Hanen Centre Publications (www.hanen.org).

Umansky, K. *Three Tapping Teddies: Musical Stories and Chants for the Very Young.* London: A&C Black.

KEY POINTS *for early social play*	
WHAT?	**HOW?**
Early Social Play (Reactive)	People games – social routines
Early Social Play (Reciprocal)	Joint action routines
Joint attention	EarlyBird and Hanen programmes
	Intensive interaction
	Music interaction therapy
	Proximal communication
	Picture Exchange Communication System (PECS)
	Voice Output Communication Aids (VOCA)

Unoccupied or Preoccupied

All children spend some of their play time seemingly unoccupied. This is part of routine development and may serve several purposes, including daydreaming, information processing and internal rehearsal. However, children who spend most of their time alone and unoccupied can be very difficult to engage. For these children the following strategies may be useful:

1. Work on the skills of early social play, as described in the preceding section, particularly joint attention.

2. Use the child's special interests to develop joint attention. Completing the 'Independent Play – Preoccupied' section of the SPR Assessment will help to identify the child's particular interests.

3. Engage in the child's special interests alongside him or her before attempting to engage *with* the child. Aim first to share the child's experience of pleasure. Work on sharing special interests with an adult, then for a brief time with a peer.

4. Teach observer skills, as detailed in the 'Peer Play' section.

5. Develop the cognitive complexity of independent play. Teach activities from the Small Steps sections for independent functional play and independent constructional play (Appendix 3, pp.109 and 110). Having some knowledge of how to play is a prerequisite for participating in peer play.

6. ICT activities may also be a good starting point, especially if these involve the child's favourite characters. (A practical resource is Hardy *et al.*, 2002: details in the Resources section below)

7. Musical activities are often effective in engaging a child who is difficult to reach.

Resources for children who seem unoccupied or preoccupied:

Bean, J. and Oldfield, A. (2001) *Pied Piper: Musical Activities to Develop Basic Skills.* London: Jessica Kingsley Publishers.

Berger, D. (2002) *Music Therapy, Sensory Integration and the Autistic Child.* London: Jessica Kingsley Publishers.

Corke, M. (2002) *Approaches to Communication Through Music.* London: David Fulton Publishers.

Hardy, C., Ogden, J., Newman, J. and Cooper, S. (2002) *Autism and ICT: A Guide for Teachers and Parents.* London: David Fulton Publishers.

MacDonald, J. (2004) *Communicating Partners.* London: Jessica Kingsley Publishers.

Moor, J. (2002) *Playing, Laughing and Learning with Children on the Autism Spectrum: A Practical Resource of Play Ideas for Parents and Carers.* London: Jessica Kingsley Publishers.

Streeter, E. (2001) *Making Music with the Young Child with Special Needs: A Guide for Parents.* London: Jessica Kingsley Publishers.

Weiss, M. and Harris, S. (2001) *Reaching Out, Joining In: Teaching Social Skills to Young Children with Autism.* Bethesda, MD: Woodbine House.

Independent Play

Play involves social and cognitive dimensions. Research shows that both these aspects are unusual and less well developed in the play of children with autistic spectrum disorders compared with their routinely developing peers. Invariably practitioners will need to develop social and cognitive play skills and also teach others how to include children with autism in their activities. It may be necessary to work on the cognitive aspects first in order to support peer play. It is of little use teaching the child social strategies to join another's activity if he or she lacks the cognitive skills to play the actual game. As Wolfberg (1999) states, such inexperienced players are soon rejected.

Develop the *cognitive* levels at which the child is able to play independently (or with minimal support) before attempting to introduce the same activity with a play partner. Gradually increase the social complexity of the child's play by involving other children. Remember to keep within the child's social tolerance. Conversely, when teaching the social aspects of play, reduce the *cognitive* demands of the game. Begin with play activities that the child has already mastered and invite a supportive, experienced peer to join in. This will help the child to learn and practise social strategies without becoming overloaded by the actual game.

Strategies to develop cognitive play

Three areas need to be addressed: *object play, imaginative play* and *role play*. A child who merely spins the wheels of toy cars will make a less interesting playmate than one who rolls cars down a ramp, pushes them around a roadway mat, makes a traffic queue, pretends to fill up with petrol, or role plays the emergency services in an accident scenario. If the child has a special interest, such as dinosaurs or trains, use this to maintain interest and motivation.

The first step is to extend the cognitive complexity of object play by increasing the range of toys with which the child plays and developing more varied use of toys and equipment. Practical activities for developing *object play* are given in the Small Steps section under Independent Play (Appendix 3).

RESOURCES FOR DEVELOPING COGNITIVE PLAY

Beyer, J. and Gammeltoft, L. (2000) *Autism and Play*. London: Jessica Kingsley Publishers.

Behavioural Intervention Association (no date) *Embracing Play: Teaching your Child with Autism.* (video) Chesterfield: Winslow Press.

Moor, J. (2002) *Playing, Laughing and Learning with Children on the Autism Spectrum: A Practical Resource of Play Ideas for Parents and Carers.* London: Jessica Kingsley Publishers.

Pretence and role play

The second step is to teach *pretence* and *role play*. Imaginative play and role play help children develop non-literal thinking and begin to understand others' perspectives – important skills for children with autistic spectrum disorders to learn. Teach pretend play skills using 'absent objects' and 'substitute objects' where one object represents another: for example, a box used as a pretend garage. Teach play scripts for roles within familiar stories or scenarios. Small

Steps guidance and sample session plans for teaching imaginative and role play are included in Appendices 2 and 3.

RESOURCES FOR DEVELOPING PRETENCE AND ROLE PLAY

Howlin, P., Baron-Cohen, S. and Hadwin, J. (1999) *Teaching Children with Autism to Mind-Read.* Chichester: Wiley.

Jordan, R. and Libby, S. (1997) 'Developing and Using Play in the Curriculum.' In S. Powell and R. Jordan (eds) *Autism and Learning: A Guide to Good Practice.* London: David Fulton Publishers.

Lear, R. (1996) *Play Helps: Toys & Activities for Children with Special Needs.* Chesterfield: Winslow Press.

Longhorn, F. (1999) *Sensory Drama for Very Special People.* Wootton: Catalyst Education Resources.

Sherratt, D. and Peter, M. (2002) *Developing Play and Drama in Children with Autistic Spectrum Disorders.* London: David Fulton Publishers.

Stagnitti, K. (2002) *Learn to Play.* Chesterfield: Winslow Press.

Wolfberg, P. (1999) *Play and Imagination in Children with Autism.* New York: Teachers College Press.

Strategies to help children develop from independent to peer play

1. Work on observer skills (see 'Peer Play' section).

2. Develop the child's tolerance of the proximity (nearness) of others – first one peer, then a pair of children. Progress to a small group and then to a larger group. Begin by positioning the child at the outer edge of groups.

3. Work on tolerance of other children coming and going.

4. Work on tolerance of peers changing their activities.

5. Work on parallel play and imitation (see 'Peer Play' section).

6. Teach peers strategies for including the child with autism in their play. For structured approaches look at:

    Adams, J. (1995) 'Peer coaching.' In J. Adams (1995) *Autism and PDD: Creative Ideas During the School Years.* Chesterfield: Winslow Press.

    Greenberg, J. (2005) *Fostering Peer Interaction in Early Childhood Settings.* Chesterfield: Winslow Press.

    Newton, C., Taylor, G. and Wilson, D. (1996) 'Circles of friends.' *Educational Psychology in Practice 11*, 4.

    Whittaker, P., Barratt, P., Joy, H., Potter, M. and Thomas, G. (1998) 'Children with autism and peer group support: Using circles of friends.' *British Journal of Special Education 25*, 2, 60–64.

    Wolfberg, P. (2005) *Peer Play and the Autistic Spectrum.* Chesterfield: Winslow Press.

7. Check out PSHE, RE, PE and music curriculum resources for circle time activities. Practical resources include:

    Barratt, P., Border, J., Joy, H., Parkinson, A., Potter, M. and Thomas, G. (2000) *Developing Pupils' Social Communication Skills.* London: David Fulton Publishers.

Corke, M. (2002) *Approaches to Communication Through Music.* London: David Fulton Publishers.

Mosley, J. and Sonnet, H. (2001) *Here We Go Round: Quality Circle Time for 3–5 year olds.* Trowbridge: Positive Press.

Nash, M. (2002) *Language Development: Circle Time Sessions to Improve Communication Skills.* London: David Fulton Publishers.

Sher, B. (1995) *Popular Games for Positive Play.* Chesterfield: Winslow Press.

KEY POINTS *for stepping from independent to peer play*

When teaching new play skills, separate out the cognitive and social aspects. Teach each aspect separately.

Introduce a supportive experienced player.

Build up from individual coaching to a peer-pair and then a small group but keep within the child's social tolerance.

Peer Play

> Playground, a sacred place, where dreams run wild.
> Where the wise educator can understand a child.
>
> (Source unknown)

Through play with peers children develop the foundation skills for forming relationships, managing conflict and acquiring social and cultural values. For most children, playtime provides a welcome break from the pressures of academic work. However, autobiographies of individuals with autistic spectrum disorders (ASDs) frequently describe these unstructured breaks as a time of confusion, fear and social isolation, with refuge sought in solitary ritualistic activity (Sainsbury, 2000). Research has identified that isolated children and those perceived as 'different' run the highest risk of exploitation and bullying (Gray, 2002). Personal accounts by those with ASD often portray this. What preventive measures can parents and practitioners put in place? A combination of direct teaching, structured practice and supported play is often effective. Strategies include:

1. Explicit teaching of skills or strategies: for example, socially acceptable ways of entering peer play. Teach the child to recognise positive overtures from peers and how to respond to them. Teach peers how to recognise and accept the sometimes unorthodox approaches of the child with social communication difficulties (see previous section for interventions and resources).

2. Written and/or picture scripts (using photos, pictures or symbols) to explicitly teach the child when to say and how to do what. Specific examples are given in the appendices. Use Social Stories, play scripts

and video. Observe the interaction of typically developing children in the child's group. What strategies do they use? What phrases to enter, maintain and leave their play with others? Make sure that the skills you teach will be appropriate to the child's peer group.

3. Structured practice: to begin with, provide activities with a structured format, such as board games, computer games or playground games (e.g. *Duck, Duck, Goose* or *Farmer in the Den*). These offer opportunities to experience peer play in more predictable and therefore less stressful contexts.

4. Supported play: work from rehearsal and structured practice to visual prompting in situ, then monitoring. Gradually reduce the levels of support and prompting as the child's competency grows.

5. The option to stay in at playtime with a preferred peer or peer buddy.

6. Peer tutoring from 'expert players', a peer buddy or circle of friends.

Stages of peer play

The four stages of peer play are Observer, Parallel Play, Associative Play and Co-operative/Co-ordinated Play. Use of the Social Play Record Assessment will identify the type(s) of peer play in which a child usually engages. Strategies are suggested for developing social play at each of these stages and for moving play forward to the next stage. A list of recommended resources follows.

OBSERVER

When is a child ready to interact with others? Observer behaviours of watching, copying and proximity are indices of readiness for social play with peers. To develop skills at and on from this stage use the following strategies:

1. Develop tolerance of the proximity of others.

2. Encourage the child to watch his or her peers from within speaking distance.

3. Teach the child to imitate (see Small Steps, Appendix 3, for guidance).

4. Begin to teach *entry* strategies: for example, greeting peers by name and playing alongside others.

PARALLEL PLAY

To develop skills at and on from this stage use the following strategies:

1. Continue working on imitation (see Small Steps for guidance).

2. Work on tolerance of peers comings and goings.

3. Work on tolerance of peers' changes of activity.

4. Develop more varied use of toys/equipment (see 'Independent Play' section).

5. Encourage the child to speak to peers: for example, to greet by name, to ask for toys.

ASSOCIATIVE PLAY

This is an important transition stage. Children with autistic spectrum disorders often need to develop *associative* play skills before they can learn to play co-operatively with peers. To develop skills at and on from this stage use the following strategies:

1. Work on positive responses to peers' approaches.

2. Work on sharing a box of toys, whilst *maintaining own set*.

3. Work on *exchanging* toys/equipment (swap so each child retains something).

4. Work on when and how to take turns. This is more difficult than *exchanging* toys because when it is not his or her turn the child may have to wait with nothing or with a toy or activity he or she does not want. Use *visual* prompts to mark turns: for example, a 'Wait' card; checklists (names or photos) for whose turn is next; sand-timers to show how long turns last.

5. Begin work on conflict resolution.

6. Work on transition between activities.

7. Help the child to begin to develop a mutual friendship through *shared interests*. These often involve fairly basic physical games at first, such as running around the playground with one or two peers or playing on the climbing frame. Play may progress to specific interests such as trains, dinosaurs or collecting items, sports activities (e.g. bowling, swimming) or computer games. *Mutual friendship* is defined by maintaining proximity, spending 30 per cent or more time with and sharing positive affect (smiling and laughing) with a peer.

CO-OPERATIVE / CO-ORDINATED PLAY

To develop skills at and on from this stage use the following strategies:

1. Teach strategies to *maintain* play: for example, sharing, taking turns, consulting others, offering and accepting suggestions, dealing with conflict and disagreement, reconciliation.

2. Develop play sequences of several steps, based on familiar themes.

3. Work on mutual goals: planning, negotiating and executing.

4. Work on role play, using characters and themes from real-life, familiar stories and imaginary events.

5. Work on emotional regulation, i.e. recognition, understanding and appropriate expression of own feelings. Link to consequences of actions.

6. Work on empathy: recognition of and appropriate responses to others' needs, feelings and perspectives.

7. Teach scripts for exiting peer play: for example, 'I'm off now!' or 'See you later!'

8. Teach strategies for avoiding peer play and for coping with rejection by peers.

9. Work on the concept of 'friends'. Teach skills for making and sustaining friendships (see 'Friendship Skills' section and Small Steps in Appendix 3).

Resources for developing peer play

Adams, J. (1993) *The Buddy System and Peer Coaching in Autism – PDD: Creative Ideas During the School Years.* Ontario: Adams Publications.

Amos, J. and Spenceley, A. (1999) *Growing Up Series: Making Friends.* Publishing Evans Group (www.evansbooks.co.uk). (Also in this series: *Being Kind; Being Helpful; Owning Up; Sharing; Taking Turns.*)

Barratt, P., Border, J., Joy, H., Parkinson, A., Potter, M. and Thomas, G. (2000) *Developing Pupils' Social Communication Skills.* London: David Fulton Publishers.

Fuge, G. and Berry, R. (2004) *Pathways to Play.* Chesterfield: Winslow Press.

Gray, C. (2000) *The New Social Story Book.* Chesterfield: Winslow Press (www.the graycenter.org).

Greenberg, J. (2005) *Fostering Peer Interaction in Early Childhood Settings.* Hanen Teacher Talk Series. Chesterfield: Winslow Press.

Gregson, B. (1982) *The Incredible Indoor Games Book.* Chesterfield: Winslow Press.

Gregson, B. (1982) *The Outrageous Outdoor Games Book.* Chesterfield: Winslow Press.

Hannah, L. (2001) *Teaching Young Children with Autistic Spectrum Disorders: A Practical Guide for Parents and Staff in Mainstream Schools and Nurseries.* London: National Autistic Society Publications.

Jordan, R. and Libby, S. (1997) 'Developing and using play in the curriculum.' In S. Powell and R. Jordan (eds) *Autism and Learning: A Guide to Good Practice.* London: David Fulton Publishers.

Kelly, A. (2003) *Talkabout Activities: Developing Social Communication Skills.* Chesterfield: Winslow Press.

Macintyre, C. (2001) *Enhancing Learning through Play. A Developmental Perspective for Early Years Settings.* London: David Fulton Publishers.

Macintyre, C. (2002) *Play for Children with Special Needs.* London: David Fulton Publishers.

Mosley, J. and Thorpe, G. (2000) *All Year Round: Exciting Ideas for Peaceful Playtimes.* Great Horwood: Incentive Plus.

Moyes, R. (2003) *Incorporating Social Goals in the Classroom.* London: Jessica Kingsley Publishers.

Nicholls, S. (1992) *Bobby Shaftoe, Clap your Hands.* London: A&C Black.

Powell, H. (2001) *Game-Songs.* London: A&C Black Publications (www.acblack.com)

Reese, P. and Challenner, N. (2002) *Autism and PDD: Social Skills Lessons.* Chesterfield: Winslow Press.

Rinaldi, W. (1992) *The Social Use of Language Programme.* Windsor: Nfer-Nelson.

Rinaldi, W. (1993) *The Social Use of Language Programme: Primary & Pre-school Teaching Pack.* Chilworth: Rinaldi.

Schroeder, A. (2001) *Time to Talk.* Leicester: Taskmaster.

Sherratt, D. and Peter, M. (2002) *Developing Play and Drama in Children with Autistic Spectrum Disorders.* London: David Fulton Publishers.

Sussman, F. (1999) *More Than Words Program.* Toronto: Hanen Centre Publications.

Weitzman, E. (1992) *Learning Language and Loving It.* Toronto: Hanen Centre Publications.

Wolfberg, P. (2005) *Peer Play and the Autistic Spectrum.* Chesterfield: Winslow Press.

KEY POINTS *for peer play*	
WHAT?	**HOW?**
Observer skills	Develop tolerance of parallel and associative play before introducing co-operative play.
Entry strategies	
Maintenance strategies, including how to play	Utilise structured play activities with a consistent format, e.g. board games.
Conflict resolution	When introducing new games, teach cognitive and social aspects separately.
Exit strategies	
Avoiding peer play	Gradually reduce the level of support and prompting.

Advanced Group Play

Advanced group play consolidates and extends the skills needed for interaction within larger and more socially demanding groups and for functioning as part of a team. At this stage children are learning to identify with peer groups, to work and play collaboratively, to develop their communication and conversation skills, to control their emotions, to use a range of strategies for resolving conflicts, to apply rules more flexibly, to cope with competition and to understand leadership. These skills are fundamental to the development of positive relationships on an interpersonal level, in the workplace and within the wider community.

Skills to develop at this stage of social play

1. Teach more sophisticated entry skills, including peer group *identity* to enable the child to fit in. Look at dress code, vocabulary, activities, gadgets, awareness of music/fashion/sports icons.

2. Teach maintenance skills, including group participation; control of emotions; strategies for negotiation, compromise, persuasion, assertion and reconciliation.

3. Work on empathy and consequences of actions.

4. Work on team games: team identity; applying and adapting rules; strategies for coping with competition, winning and losing. Using *first/second/third* instead of *winner/loser* may be easier for the children to accept to begin with. Consider team games other than sports, which demand physical as well as social prowess. Physical difficulties (e.g. with co-ordination and timing) are not uncommon in individuals with autistic spectrum disorders. Sports activities may

provoke high stress levels and also place the child at risk of rejection by more able team mates.

5. Teach more sophisticated exit skills.

6. See Small Steps (Appendix 3) and the resources list at the end of the 'Friendship Skills' section for specific activities.

KEY POINTS *for advanced group play*	
WHAT?	**HOW?**
Peer identity	Develop understanding of belonging to a group and sense of community.
Control of emotions	
Team games	Utilise resources for PHSE, RE, PE, circle time and assemblies.
Flexible rule application	
Strategies for negotiation, persuasion and reconciliation	Teach 'how to' through Social Stories and Comic Strip Conversations (www.thegraycenter.org).
	Utilise social skills programmes like the *Social Use of Language Programme* (Rinaldi, 1992 and 1993), *Social Skills Training* and *The Social Skills Picture Book* (Baker, 2003) and *Social Skills Programmes* (Aarons and Gittens, 2003) – see the Resources section at the end of the Friendship Skills section.

Friendship Skills

Friendships are an important route to social understanding and inclusion, to support networks and to mental and physical well-being. Friendships begin to develop alongside other types of social play from around the age of two so it is important to start work on these skills as soon as possible. Friendships may develop for a variety of reasons but early friendships are often formed on the basis of familiarity and similar interests. Friendship skills may be addressed as follows:

1. Work on skills for making friends (see Small Steps in Appendix 3), which will include:

   • the 'feel good' factor: experiencing fun activities with peers who are in regular contact with the child with social interaction needs. Work from activities the child prefers and enjoys. Physical play is often popular with young children.

   • exploring the concept of friendship: what friends do and don't do; what makes a good friend. Avoid over-generalizing, e.g. 'We can all be friends!' Typically developing children have just two or three mutual friends.

2. Develop skills to *sustain* friendships (see Small Steps), which include:

   - sharing similar interests

   - social and emotional empathy (e.g. friends like each other, show concern for each other)

   - offering and receiving help

   - giving and receiving compliments and criticism

   - conflict resolution

   - recognising mistakes and how to apologise

   - conversation skills and interactional style

   - humour (e.g. riddles, jokes, sayings).

3. Teach how to handle rejection of and by others, including the transient nature of friendships and how to recognise, deal with and prevent bullying and exploitation. Sainsbury's (2000) research found that bullying and teasing are almost invariably part of the school experience for children with autistic spectrum disorders.

4. Develop peers' understanding, tolerance and inclusion of the child.

The Small Steps for advanced group play and friendship skills (Appendix 3) give detailed targets. Remember that many of these skills may be difficult for children with social communication needs. It is a huge step from learning about the requisite skills to using them in real-life situations. In addition to teaching the children specific social skills, practitioners will need to address others' attitudes and explore ways of adapting the social environment to maximise the possibilities for enjoyment and success.

One of the best ways to practise skills at these stages of social play is for the child to join a club or group that focuses on his or her special interest or particular talents (e.g. computers, music, photography, sci-fi, swimming) or that has a caring ethos (cubs, guides, after-school club). It may be helpful to be supported by a peer buddy or a 'befriender'. In some areas, autistic societies or social services run supported play and befriender schemes.

KEY POINTS for friendship skills	
WHAT?	**HOW?**
Concept of friendship	Work from familiarity and similar interests.
Control of emotions	Set up a friendship group or friends club.
How to make friends	Utilise PHSE, RE and music resources.
How to keep friends	Use stories and activities from social skills programmes (see resources below).
True or false friend (dealing with bullying and exploitation)	Use Social Stories and Comic Strip Conversations (www.thegraycenter.org).
	Consider the 'Circles of Friends' approach.
	Consider a peer buddy or peer tutoring.
	Look into 'befriender' schemes.

Specific resources for advanced group play and friendship skills are suggested below. Curriculum resources for PSHE, RE, PE and music, especially those for circle time, contain useful activities for working on these skills.

Resources for advanced group play and friendship skills

SOCIAL SKILLS

Aarons, M. and Gittens, T. (1998) *Autism: A Social Skills Approach for Children and Adolescents.* Leicester: Taskmaster.

Aarons, M. and Gittens, T. (2003) *Social Skills Programmes: An Integrated Approach from Early Years to Adolescence.* Leicester: Taskmaster.

Adams, J. (1997) *Autism–PDD: More Creative Ideas, From Age Eight to Early Adulthood.* Ontario: Adams Publications.

Baker, J. (2003) *Social Skills Training.* Shawnee Mission, KS: Autism Asperger Publishing Company.

Baker, J. (2003) *The Social Skills Picture Book.* Arlington, TX: Future Horizons, Inc.

Early, Intermediate and Advanced Social Skills Posters. Great Horwood: Incentive Plus.

Gajewski, N., Hirn, P. and Mayo, P. (1998) *Social Skills Strategies.* Chesterfield: Winslow Press.

Gray, C. (1994) *Comic Strip Conversations.* Chesterfield: Winslow Press.

Gray, C. (1997) *Social Stories and Comic Strip Conversations Video.* Chesterfield: Winslow Press.

Gray C. (2000) *The New Social Story Book.* Chesterfield: Winslow Press.

Kelly, A. (2003) *Talkabout Activities: Developing Social Communication Skills.* Leicester: Taskmaster.

Rinaldi, W. (1992) *Social Use of Language Programme.* Windsor: Nfer-Nelson.

Rinaldi, W. (1993) *Social Use of Language Programme: Primary & Pre-school Teaching Pack.* Chilworth: Rinaldi.

Searle, Y. and Streng, I. (1996) *The Social Skills Game.* London: Jessica Kingsley Publishers.

Schroeder, A. (1996) *Socially Speaking.* Leicester: Taskmaster.

Schroeder, A. (2003) The Socially Speaking Game. Leicester: Taskmaster.

Smith, C. (2003) *Writing and Developing Social Stories.* Chesterfield: Winslow Press.

SOCIO-EMOTIONAL SKILLS

Baron-Cohen, S. (2004) *Mind Reading: The Interactive Guide to Emotions.* London: Jessica Kingsley Publishers.

Buron, K. (2003) *When My Autism Gets Too Big!* London: National Autistic Society Publications.

Doherty, K., McNally, P. and Sherrard, E. (2003) *I have Autism… What's that?* London: National Autistic Society Publications.

Howlin, P., Baron-Cohen, S. and Hadwin, J. (1999) *Teaching Children with Autism to Mind-Read. A Practical Guide.* Chichester: Wiley.

Kelly, A. (2003) *Talkabout Relationships.* Leicester: Taskmaster.

Sher, B. (1998) *Self-Esteem Games.* Chesterfield: Winslow Press.

Keable, D. (no date) The Mad Sad Glad Game. Chesterfield: Winslow Press.

Thorpe, P. (2004) *Understanding Difficulties at Break Time and Lunchtime: Guidelines for Pupils with Autistic Spectrum Disorders.* London: National Autistic Society Publications.

FRIENDSHIP SKILLS

Braithwaite, A. (2001) *Choices: Being Friends.* London: A&C Black.

Braithwaite, A. (2001) *Feeling Angry.* London: A&C Black.

Braithwaite, A. (2001) *Feeling Shy.* London: A&C Black.

Braithwaite, A. (2001) *Feeling Sad.* London: A&C Black.

Andersen-Wood, L. and Smith, B. (1997) *Working with Pragmatics.* Chesterfield: Winslow Press.

Brown, L. and Brown M. (1998) *How to be a Friend.* New York: Little, Brown.

Gutstein, S. and Sheely, K. (2002) *Relationship Development Intervention with Young Children: Social and Emotional Development Activities for Asperger Syndrome, Autism, PDD and NLD.* London: Jessica Kingsley Publishers.

Gutstein, S. and Sheely, K. (2002) *Relationship Development Intervention with Children, Adolescents and Adults: Social and Emotional Development Activities for Asperger Syndrome, Autism, PDD and NLD.* London: Jessica Kingsley Publishers.

Hurley-Geffner, E. (1995) 'Friendships between children with and without disabilities.' In R.L. Koegel and L.K. Koegel (eds) *Teaching Children with Autism: Strategies for Initiating Positive Interaction and Improving Learning Opportunities.* Baltimore, MD: Paul Brookes.

Jordan, R. and Jones, G. (1999) *Meeting the Needs of Children with Autistic Spectrum Disorders.* London: David Fulton Publishers.

Murrell, D. (2001) *Tobin Learns to Make Friends.* Chesterfield: Winslow Press.

Rogers, R. (1996) *Making Friends.* New York: Putnam and Grosset.

Rubin, K. (2002) *The Friendship Factor.* New York: Plenum Press.

TEACCH Organisation (www.unc.edu/depts/teacch).

PEER SUPPORT

Adams, J. (1995) 'Buddy system and peer coaching.' In J. Adams *Autism-PDD: Creative Ideas During the School Years.* Ontario: Adams Publishing.

Davies, J. (no date) *Children with Autism: A Booklet for Brothers and Sisters.* Child Development Research Unit, University of Nottingham. Available from National Autistic Society Publications.

Newton, C. Taylor, G. and Wilson, D. (1996) 'Circles of Friends.' *Educational Psychology in Practice 11,* 4.

Taylor, G. (1998) 'Community building in schools: developing a circle of friends.' *Educational and Child Psychology 14,* 45–50.

Telmo, I. (2004) *Play with Me: Including Children with Autism in Mainstream Primary Schools.* London: National Autistic Society Publications.

Whitaker, P., Barratt, P., Joy, H., Potter, M. and Thomas, G. (1998) 'Children with autism and peer group support: Using circles of friends'. *British Journal of Special Education 25,* 2, 60–64.

GROUP GAMES

Barratt, P., Border, J., Joy, H. and Parkinson, A. (2000) *Developing Pupils' Social Communication Skills.* London: David Fulton Publishers.

Gregson, B. (1982) *The Incredible Indoor Games Book.* Chesterfield: Winslow Press.

Gregson, B. (1982) *The Outrageous Outdoor Games Book.* Chesterfield: Winslow Press.

Mosley, J. and Sonnet, H. (2003) *101 Games for Social Skills.* Leicester: Taskmaster.

Mosley, J. and Thorpe, G. (2002) *All Year Round: Exciting Ideas for Peaceful Playtimes.* Great Horwood: Incentive Plus.

CIRCLE TIME

Mosley, J. (1996) *Circle Time: Photocopiable Materials for Use with the Jenny Mosley Circle Time Model.* Trowbridge: Positive Press.

Mosley, J. (2001) *Quality Circle Time in the Primary Classroom.* London: David Fulton Publishers.

Mosley, J. and Tew, M. (1999) *Quality Circle Time in the Secondary School.* London: David Fulton Publishers.

Nash, M. (2002) *Language Development: Circle Time Sessions to Improve Communication Skills.* London: David Fulton Publishers.

ASPERGER SYNDROME

Attwood, T. (1998) *Asperger's Syndrome: A Guide for Parents and Professionals.* London: Jessica Kingsley Publishers.

Boyd, B. (2003) *Parenting a Child with Asperger Syndrome.* London: Jessica Kingsley Publishers.

Cumine, V., Leach, J. and Stevenson, G. (1998) *Asperger Syndrome: A Practical Guide for Teachers.* London: David Fulton Publishers.

Faherty, C. (2000) *Asperger's: What Does It Mean to Me?* Chesterfield: Winslow Press.

Gray, C. (1997) 'Pictures of me – introducing students with Asperger syndrome to their talents, personality and diagnosis.' *Communication,* Winter.

Ives, M. (2001) *What is Asperger Syndrome and How Will it Affect Me? A Guide for Young People.* London: National Autistic Society Publications.

Leicester City and County Councils (1998) *Asperger Syndrome: Practical Strategies for the Classroom. A Teacher's Guide.* London: National Autistic Society Publications.

Sainsbury, C. (2000) *Martian in the Playground.* Bristol: Lucky Duck.

Stuart-Hamilton, I. (2004) *An Asperger Dictionary of Everyday Expressions.* London: Jessica Kingsley Publishers.

Welton, J. (2004) *Can I Tell you about Asperger Syndrome? A Guide for Friends and Family.* London: Jessica Kingsley Publishers.

Conclusion

Social play is a priority route to social inclusion.

Social play has long been identified as a primary social and cultural activity for acquiring symbolic capacity, interpersonal skills and social knowledge (Vygotsky 1978). All children have a right to access the knowledge, skills, opportunities and experiences that lead to such social competence. Studies have identified the impact of difficulties in social play on development and learning, on long-term adjustment, on health and quality of life, and on the whole family's inclusion in society. Studies have also linked social play to wider social and economic objectives, recognising the contribution play can make to reducing crime and antisocial behaviour (Department of Media, Culture and Sport 2004). Functional assessment, well-targeted intervention and positive social experiences should be a routine component of educational provision for children with autistic spectrum disorders or any other form of social interaction difficulty. A growing body of research (see Appendix 4) shows that with appropriate support these children can and do make qualitative and quantitative gains in social play.

The purpose of the Social Play Record is to provide an assessment and intervention framework for systematically evaluating, monitoring and developing social interaction through play. The Social Play Record does not presume to offer an easy route, but it does provide a structured, longitudinal approach to assessment and intervention within a complex area of development. Children with social interaction difficulties are likely to need long-term support with social play. Strategies should be tailored to individual learning needs, adapting and changing over time to match maturation and skill development. This demands a variety of resources from which to draw. The Social Play Record offers approaches, strategies, activities and resources for each type of social play, together with Small Steps guidance for target setting. It also addresses others' attitudes and the social learning environment. It is founded on a comprehensive review of well-substantiated literature, reflecting empirical thinking and best practice. The suggestions are not prescriptive but do represent a selection of good-practice interventions. Practitioners and parents will undoubtedly discover others and will develop their own approaches and resources. They will surely find intervention through social play a fascinating, productive and fun way to help children develop the social interaction skills that are so essential for inclusion in society.

Appendix 1
Worked examples from the SPR Assessment

Social Play Record Assessment

PEER PLAY

Extent of social participation

Key elements: As described in boxes below.

Name: Kyle   Date: Feb. 05

TYPE OF PEER PLAY AND KEY MARKERS	ASSESSMENT RATING				COMMENTS
	Often	Sometimes	When prompted	Needs to work on	Describe context and how it affects child
OBSERVER					
A. Watches peers from within speaking distance.	☑	☐	☐	☐	
B. Comments on peers' activity.	☑	☐	☐	☐	
C. Turns towards peers.	☐	☐	☑	☐	
PARALLEL					
A. Plays alongside peers but independently.	☑	☐	☐	☐	
B. Copies peers.	☑	☐	☐	☐	
C. Looks and smiles at those he or she is copying.	☑	☐	☐	☐	
ASSOCIATIVE					
A. Responds positively to peers' approaches.	☑	☐	☐	☐	
B. Exchanges or shares materials.	☑	☐	☐	☐	
C. Speaks to peers.	☐	☐	☑	☐	
CO-OPERATIVE					
A. Shares materials and activities or goals, taking turns.	☑	☐	☐	☐	Sequenced play with cars — contributed to story line.
B. Offers suggestions for attaining goals or for extending play themes.	☐	☐	☑	☐	
C. Complements and exchanges roles.	☐	☐	☐	☑	

Social Play Record Assessment

PEER PLAY

Play preferences

Name: Kyle   Date: Feb. 05

MATERIALS, TOYS OR ACTIVITIES	PEERS	CONTEXTS (THEMES AND SETTINGS)
Cars. Train. Chase / running but <u>not</u> 'Tiggy'.	Familiar peers e.g. classmates. More able peers.	Indoor and outdoor play in familiar settings but reticent in new / unfamiliar contexts.

Social Play Record Assessment

PEER PLAY

Social Play tasks and strategies

Name: Kyle   Date: Feb. 05

Describe social play *strategies* the child uses and rate their frequency.
Scores: often = 3; sometimes = 2; when prompted = 1; rarely or never = 0

SOCIAL PLAY TASKS	APPROPRIATE AND EFFECTIVE STRATEGIES	INAPPROPRIATE OR INEFFECTIVE STRATEGIES	NEEDS TO WORK ON
A. Entering peer play	• Plays alongside • Copies • Looks at	• Doesn't speak to peers unless prompted.	✓
B. Maintaining peer play	• Asks for toys (doesn't take)	• Dislikes sharing	✓
C. Resolving peer conflict		• Screams "No!"	✓
D. Exiting peer play		• Just wanders off	✓
E. Avoiding peer play	• Verbally, e.g. "I do this on my own!"		

Social Play Record Assessment

FRIENDSHIP SKILLS

Key elements: Acceptance and rejection of and by peers. Understanding of 'friendship' develops. Formation and maintenance of relationships.

Name: Kyle   Date: Feb. 05

KEY SOCIAL PLAY MARKERS	Often	Sometimes	When prompted	Needs to work on	COMMENTS Describe context and how it affects child (e.g. situation, peers, activities, prompts)
A. Making friends					
1. Peers accept and choose child.	☑	☐	☐	☐	
2. Child interacts with peers in preference to adults.	☑	☐	☐	☐	
3. Child has mutual friendships (i.e. laughs and smiles with friends; spends 30% time or more with; friendships lasts over time).	☐	☑	☐	☑	Monitor – emerging ?
B. Interactional style					
1. Style is appropriate to peer group.	☐	☐	☑	☐	Directs peers
C. Conversational skills					
1. Inititates conversation with peers.	☐	☐	☑	☑	
2. Listens and responds to peers.	☐	☑	☐	☐	
3. Talks with, not at peers, taking conversational turns.	☐	☑	☐	☐	
4. Ends conversation appropriately.	☐	☐	☐	☐	
D. Sustaining friendships					
1. Shows concern for friend's feelings.	☐	☑	☐	☐	
2. Shares own interests and activities.	☐	☐	☑	☑	
3. Seeks solutions to avoid or resolve conflict.	☐	☑	☐	☐	
4. Accommodates friend's preferences, interests, needs.	☐	☐	☐	☐	
5. Offers and seeks practical support; e.g. lends/shares items, helps, advises, defends.	☐	☐	☐	☐	
6. Shares experiences, feelings, secrets, humour.	☐	☐	☐	☐	

Social Play Record Assessment

Social Play Record Assessment

PRACTITIONER RATING OF PEER RELATIONSHIPS

Name: Kyle   Date: Feb. 05

A. CHILD'S RESPONSE TO PEERS:

Tick box as appropriate

SOLITARY: Child is disinterested/withdrawn/actively avoids contact with peers.

☑ Never or rarely   □ Sometimes   □ Often

HESITANT: Child is shy/socially immature (inept entry skills; fumbled attempts).

□ Never or rarely   ☑ Sometimes   □ Often

ACTIVE: Child is sociable.

□ Never or rarely   □ Prompted   ☑ Sometimes   □ Often

FRIENDSHIPS:

☑ Child has no mutual friends.

□ Child has one mutual friend.

□ Child has more than one mutual friend.

B. PEERS' RESPONSE TO CHILD

A completed example is shown in Appendix I.

Reject	50%		Accept
Isolate		X	Invite to join
Actively avoid			Offer toys or materials
Show hostility			Assign roles or tasks
Mock or bully			
Ignore			**Acknowledge**
Indifferent		X	Smile
Disinterested			Greet or speak to
Tolerate			**Support**
Accept presence		X	Adapt speech/behaviour
Offer low-status role			Take responsibility for
Over-protect			Show or guide

Social Play Record Assessment

PEER PREFERENCES CHART

Name: Kyle   Date: Feb. 05

NAMES OF CHILDREN IN PEER GROUP*	LIKES TO PLAY WITH A LOT ☺	LIKES TO PLAY WITH A BIT ☺	DOES NOT LIKE TO PLAY WITH ☹	BEST FRIEND** ☺☺	EVERYDAY PLAYMATES ***
1. Oscar	✓				
2. Ben	✓			✓	
3. Sandra		✓			
4. Melinda		✓			
5. Jack			✓		
6. Martin		✓			
7. John		✓			
8. Lizzie			✓		
9.					
10.					

* Present photos individually to one child at a time. Ask: 'How much do you like to play with this person?'

** Re-present the ☺ photos. Ask: 'Who do you like to play with the most?' Place a check mark against nominated peers.

*** Present a photo of the whole group or class. Ask: 'Who do you play with most days?'

Comments:

Social Play Record Assessment

QUESTIONNAIRE ABOUT FRIENDS

Name: _███████_____ Class: __4_____

Date: 25.02.05

Circle your choice and fill in the gaps

In class I like to work:

by myself

with another person

in a group

In PE I choose __J███_____ to be my partner.

At playtime or break I like to be:

by myself

with a friend

with a group of friends

I like to play climbing frame

I don't like to play tiggy

I feel happy when people Play with me

I feel sad when people Pick on me

A friend is someone who looks out for you

My friends are B█████ G█████ Miss G████

Social Play Record Assessment

PLANNING SHEET

Name: Kyle

Date: Feb. 05

INTERVENTION TARGETS FOR SOCIAL PLAY

Target 1: To invite a peer to share his activity.

Outcome: Feb. 06

Often responds positively when familiar peers ask to join him but needs reminding to invite them. Shares toys and play themes. Accepts others' suggestions to extend the play and offers his own ideas. Negotiates and exchanges roles within familiar themes.

Target 2: To tell peers when he has finished playing or wants to play a different game.

Outcome: Feb. 06

Says when he's finished playing or doesn't want to play anymore. Says when he wants to change activities.
Suggests alternatives, e.g. " I know, let's play…", " I tell you what, let's play …"

Target 3: To participate in a team game (in preparation for Sports Day).

Outcome: Feb. 06

Participates in group games with familiar peer group (e.g. classmates) but needs support to operate as a team player. Accepts winning but not losing.

Social Play Record Assessment

SCORE FOR THE PLAY OBSERVATION SHEETS

Name: Kyle   Date: Feb. 05

TYPES OF SOCIAL PLAY	KEY SOCIAL PLAY MARKERS (Item letters are in top left corner of boxes) Scores: often = 3; sometimes = 2; when prompted = 1; rarely or never = 0					Social play score
Early social play (Reactive)	A $\frac{3}{3}$	B $\frac{3}{3}$	C $\frac{3}{3}$	D $\frac{3}{3}$		$\frac{12}{12}$
Early social play (Reciprocal)	A $\frac{3}{3}$	B $\frac{3}{3}$	C $\frac{3}{3}$	D $\frac{3}{3}$		$\frac{12}{12}$
Independent play	A $\frac{3}{3}$	B $\frac{3}{3}$	C $\frac{3}{3}$	D $\frac{3}{15}$		$\frac{12}{24}$
Peer play: Observer	A $\frac{3}{3}$	B $\frac{3}{3}$	C $\frac{1}{3}$			$\frac{7}{9}$
Peer play: Parallel	A $\frac{3}{3}$	B $\frac{3}{3}$	C $\frac{3}{3}$			$\frac{9}{9}$
Peer play: Associative	A $\frac{3}{3}$	B $\frac{3}{3}$	C $\frac{1}{3}$			$\frac{7}{9}$
Peer play: Co-operative	A $\frac{3}{3}$	B $\frac{1}{3}$	C $\frac{0}{3}$			$\frac{4}{9}$
Peer play: Strategies	A $\frac{3}{3}$	B $\frac{1}{3}$	C $\frac{0}{3}$	D $\frac{0}{3}$	E $\frac{1}{3}$	$\frac{5}{15}$
Advanced group	A $\frac{3}{3}$	B $\frac{0}{3}$	C $\frac{0}{3}$	D $\frac{2}{3}$	E $\frac{0}{3}$ F $\frac{0}{3}$	$\frac{5}{18}$
Friendship skills	A $\frac{7}{9}$	B $\frac{1}{3}$	C $\frac{5}{12}$	D $\frac{5}{18}$		$\frac{18}{42}$
					Total score	$\frac{91}{159}$

Social Play Record Assessment

SCORES FOR THE PRACTITIONER RATING, PEER PREFERENCES AND QUESTIONNAIRE ABOUT FRIENDS

Name: Kyle   Date: Feb . 05

Score for Practitioner Rating of Peer Relationships

Criteria for scoring	Score
A: Child's response to peers ACTIVE: score 0 for rarely or never; score 1 for prompted; score 2 for sometimes; score 3 for often. Entries under 'Solitary' and 'Hesitant' do not score. FRIENDSHIPS: score 0 if the child has no mutual friends; score 1 if child has one mutual friend; score 2 if child has more than one mutual friend.	$\dfrac{2}{5}$
B: Peers' response to child • Peers accept more than 50% of the time scores 1. • Peers acknowledge more than 50% of the time scores 1. • Peers support more than 50% of the times scores 1.	$\dfrac{3}{3}$
Total score	$\dfrac{5}{8}$

Score for Peer Preferences Chart

Criteria for scoring	Score
Receives more nominations on *likes to play with* than *does not like to play with*.	$\dfrac{1}{1}$
Receives no nomination on *does not like to play with*.	$\dfrac{0}{1}$
Receives a mutual *best friend* nomination.	$\dfrac{0}{1}$
Total score	$\dfrac{1}{3}$

Social Play Record Assessment

SCORE FOR THE QUESTIONNAIRE ABOUT FRIENDS

Name: Kyle   Date: Feb. 05

Score for Questionnaire about Friends

Items on the Questionnaire	Criteria for scoring	Score
In PE I choose…	Independently chooses a partner for PE or other activity.	$\frac{1}{1}$
At playtime or break I like to be …	Circles *with a friend* or *with a group of friends*.	$\frac{1}{1}$
I like to play…	Answer includes social games, i.e. games with others.	$\frac{0}{1}$
I do not like to play…	Answer does not include social games.	$\frac{0}{1}$
I feel happy when people…	Answer refers to social interaction.	$\frac{1}{1}$
I feel sad when people…	Answer refers to social interaction.	$\frac{1}{1}$
A friend is someone who…	One concept of friendship (e.g. plays with me) scores 1. Two or more concepts (e.g. shares things; helps you) scores 2. Answer includes what the child can do for a friend scores 3.	$\frac{1}{3}$
My friends are…	Names a *mutual* friend.	$\frac{0}{1}$
	Total score	$\frac{5}{10}$

Social Play Record Assessment

PROFILE OF SCORES

Name: Kyle   Date: Feb. 05

Assessment Measure	Score
Play Observation sheets	$\frac{91}{159}$
Practitioner Rating of Peer Relationships	$\frac{5}{8}$
Peer Preferences Chart	$\frac{1}{3}$
Questionnaire about Friends	$\frac{5}{10}$
Total score on the Social Play Record	$\frac{102}{180}$

A child's total score on the Social Play Record Assessment may be entered on the Progress Chart in the form of a bar chart or a line graph. An example is given in Appendix 1.

Social Play Record Assessment

PROGRESS CHART

Name: Kyla

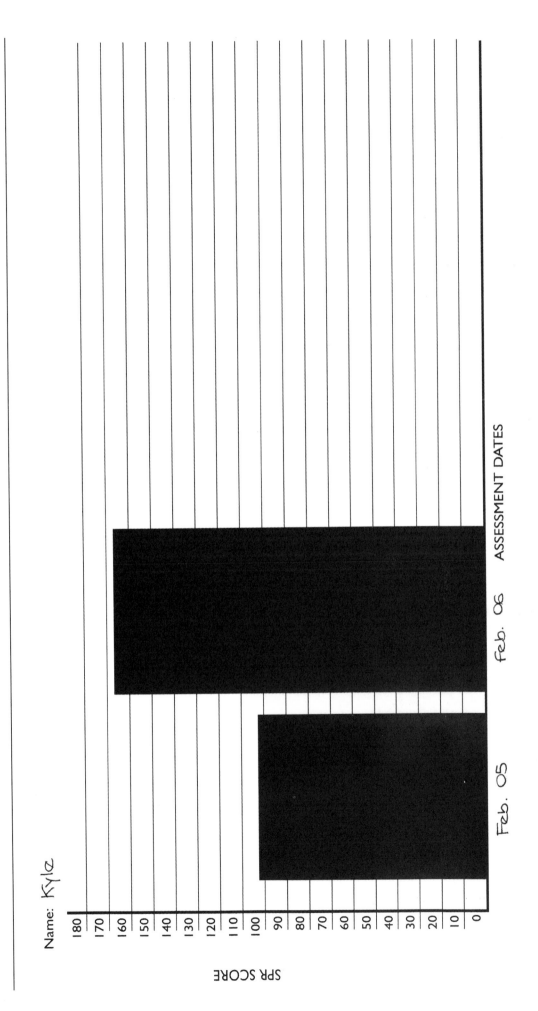

SPR SCORE

180 170 160 150 140 130 120 110 100 90 80 70 60 50 40 30 20 10 0

Feb. 05   Feb. 06   ASSESSMENT DATES

Social Play Record Assessment

SOCIAL PLAY IEP TARGETS

Name: Date:

Ask a friend to play a jigsaw.

Play a friend's game.

Play with two different people.

Say why you like a friend.

Say three things friends do.

Appendix 2

Ideas and templates for developing social play

Early Social Play and Early Object Play

1. Signal the start and end of the play session with music the child enjoys.

2. Use objects/topics of special interest to engage the child's attention.

   - Aim for imitation, for example, taking brief turns to play the drums softly and loudly, quickly and slowly, short and longer, with taps, scrapes, bangs etc.

   - Aim for sensory exploration of the objects (feel/look at/move/bang/shake/empty/fill).

   - If the child shows an interest in books, aim for him or her to follow an adult's index finger touch-pointing the pictures.

3. Self/other awareness.

   - Mirror games (*Where's X?*; funny faces; Peep-Bo; *Heads, shoulders, knees and toes*; hats).

   - Scarf or parachute games.

4. Repetitive social games.

   - Games involving tickle, pounce, chase, for example, *Round and round the garden*; *Incy Wincy Spider*.

   - *Gone!* games, e.g. hide and seek people or objects.

   - *Ready, steady, go!* games.

   - Bubbles.

5. Reciprocal play with a partner.

   - *Row your boat.*

   - *Clap your hands with me!*

   - Ball or car rolling.

6. Conventional use of *exploratory* toys.

   - Toys involving light or movement.

   - Push-button toys, e.g. animal pop-up.

- Containers to empty and fill.
- Lift-the-flap books.

7. *Constructional* play.

- Jigsaws.
- Take apart/put together toys.
- Building blocks and knocking them down.

8. *Functional* play with toys (using toys as they were intended).

- Pushing cars.
- Moving the train along the track.
- Holding telephone to ear.
- Pots and pans.

Peer Play

Aims

To develop *social* play from *parallel* play (playing alongside but not with others), through *associative* play (sharing the toys/materials) and on to *co-operative* play (sharing the materials and the task or goal).

What to do

1. Invite a preferred peer or sibling (preferably an 'expert' player who knows how to play with the toys) to join you and the focus child.

2. Begin with a *constructional* task, such as building a train track, a roadway or a tower of bricks. These activities are structured and visual, with a clear beginning and end. Add trains, cars, play people, animals to develop the play.

3. Initially the adult is the 'keeper' of the toys/materials to ensure that the children share them. The adult prompts the social aspects of sharing. At this stage the children may or may not copy each other. Encourage but don't insist on copying activities. Keep the emphasis on *sharing the materials*, not the task. Encourage the children to *exchange* toys or materials. Make sure that each child has something he or she likes from the swap. Gradually relinquish control of the materials to the children.

4. When the focus child has learnt to tolerate sharing the same set of toys with another child rather than hoarding them, move on to *sharing the task*. This marks the beginning of *co-operative play* as the children need to *take turns*. Again start with constructional activities with a strong visual structure and a clear goal. Board games (e.g.

picture lotto, Old McDonald's Farm, snakes and ladders) are also structured and visual, so are useful for teaching about turns.

5. Initially the adult controls the materials and guides the task to teach the social conventions of taking turns in play. Taking turns is difficult for many children because while they are waiting for a turn they have nothing. Holding a 'Wait' card helps children learn to wait until each player has finished his or her turn before taking theirs. Knowing if or when they will have another turn is also tricky. Represent turns visually, for example, by posting up the names or photos of the players and checking off turns as they are taken. Use sand-timers to show how long a turn lasts. Gradually relinquish control of the game to the children.

6. Teach scripts (useful phrases) for asking/inviting others to join in; exchanging or borrowing toys; taking turns; winning and losing; changing the activity; leaving the play when the child has had enough. Write these on cue cards. Rehearse beforehand and use as visual prompts during play with peers.

7. Use a visual means (e.g. a sand-timer or clock) to count down the end of play.

8. The child will probably need support (an adult or peer buddy) to transfer these skills from paired play to small groups and to different play environments.

Social and Imaginative Play

Participants

Initially the focus child and one peer, supported by an adult. Gradually increase the number of players, but stay within the child's level of social tolerance.

Materials

- Train track in box.
- Large cardboard box, felt tip pens, scissors.
- Props, for example, driver's hat, train tickets, flag, whistle, dressing-up clothes, etc. for passengers.

Activities

1. Use the train track for *constructional play*. Initially adult controls the box containing the train set to support *co-operative play* by encouraging turn-taking when choosing pieces (*sharing materials*) in order to build the track (*sharing the task*).

2. When the track is constructed, the children take turns to choose engines and carriages for a limited period of free play. Encourage the children to swap trains or accessories such as bridges (*associative play*).

3. Introduce the large cardboard box to make into an engine shed or tunnel (*pretend play – object substitution*). Discuss how to make the shed or tunnel (*collaborative problem solving*). Construct the shed or tunnel together, sharing materials and task (*co-operative play*). Incorporate what has been made into the play with the train set (*imaginative play*).

4. Use the props to introduce *imaginative role play* (driver/guard/ passengers). Model the roles as necessary. Support the child to try different roles (encourages flexibility and appreciation of others' perspectives).

5. Gradually extend the number of steps in the role play to develop *sequenced play*.

6. Develop any aspect of the play in ways that interest the child.

Imaginative Play: Object Substitution

What is object substitution?

Object substitution is a form of pretend play where objects, instead of being used according to their intended purpose, are used imaginatively to represent different things. The more dissimilar the objects are in shape, size and function, the greater the demand on the child's imagination.

Why teach this type of imaginative play?

There are three good reasons to teach this sort of play:

- to develop non-literal understanding and flexibility of thought

- to extend play skills, giving more scope for independent and social play

- to develop the creative, flexible and fun aspects of play.

Step 1: Using large objects

First identify the literal use of the object: 'What's this?' 'What is it for?' Next introduce non-literal uses for objects such as a large cardboard box, a shoebox, a piece of cloth, a cardboard tube. To begin with, offer suggestions and demonstrate them: for example, 'Let's pretend this box is a boat/car/train/plane/table/chair,' etc. 'Who wants a ride in this car?' If necessary add 'reality' props to support the children's understanding (e.g.

a steering wheel). Brainstorm uses of objects. Encourage the children to try out their ideas. Keeping to a topic (e.g. transport/furniture) helps to generate suggestions.

Step 2: Small world toys

Use familiar contexts or well-known stories and incorporate substitute objects:

- train set – use a cardboard box for a tunnel; a block of wood for the station; pieces of tissue for leaves/snow on the line; Lego bricks for the signal or crossing

- playground or park – use a small brick and cardboard to make a slide or see-saw; blue shiny paper for a duckpond; ducks made of plasticine; a round lid as a roundabout with bottle tops as seats

- garage – make a ramp, petrol pumps, roadway, road signs, traffic lights, etc.

Step 3: Role play

Use familiar contexts or well-known stories and incorporate substitute objects and dressing-up clothes. Contexts to begin with might include: a shop, café, school, magician, bus or train driver and passengers, emergency services (fire, police, ambulance, breakdown truck). You might make the props during art, design or science lessons, using non-representational construction material (Lego, Play-Doh) or 'junk' (boxes, coloured paper, straws, card).

Imaginative Sequenced Play

Aims

To develop imaginative sequenced play, in individual, paired or small group settings using:

- *object substitution:* working first from objects that are similar in function or appearance to those they are replacing, then substituting dissimilar materials

- *pretence:* working with imaginary objects, actions, feelings and properties.

What to do

Choose a play theme and *set the scene*. Work from familiar scenarios, such as getting ready for school, going shopping, making a meal. Then develop more elaborate themes: for example, a birthday party, visiting the park or fun farm, going to McDonald's. It is often helpful to read a story or look at photos of the scenario before acting it out through play.

Introduce the characters: use play people but let the children decide who they represent (mummy, birthday child, self). Encourage the children to name the characters because this will make the play narrative clearer.

Keep the materials to one side. Introduce the story *in sequence*, using only the materials for that bit of the sequence. This helps to give the play theme a *structure*, making it easier to follow. Keep the *story sequence short* to begin with, just three or four 'frames'. Try to work through the sequence from beginning to end. As confidence grows, increase the number of steps. Encourage the children to *add bits* to the story and to *change* it.

Suggest, show, think, copy: suggest one or two imaginative ways to use the materials, show the children what you mean, give them time to think about what you have demonstrated, then encourage the children to copy you. Use simple language and short phrases: 'Let's pretend!' 'I pretend this brick is a cake.' 'I pretend this leaf is a blanket.' Show what you mean at every step. Then *ask* the children for their ideas: 'What could you pretend with this box/leaf/brick?' 'How does the mummy feel?' 'What is the little boy going to do?' 'What happens next?'

When an imaginative play script has been mastered in an individual play session, *invite another child* to join in. You will still need to support the play to encourage sharing of toys/materials, taking turns, and coping with changes.

Rules for playing with a friend

Talk to each other.

Listen to each other.

Take turns.

Wait for your turn.

Look at each other.

Check your friend's face is happy.

Have fun!

✔

Scripts for playing with friends

How to join in

What to do

Stand near.

Look at faces.

Smile!

What to say

'Hello.'

'I like that.'

'Can I play?'

How to keep the play going

What to do

Take turns.

Share toys.

Tell your friends:

What to say

'Let's take turns!'

'Let's share.'

'This is good.'

How to change the game

What to do

Tell your friends:

Choose another game.

Ask your friends:

What to say

'I don't want to play this.'

'Let's play another game.'

'What do you want to play?'

How to stop

What to do

Tell your friends:

Walk away.

What to say

'I'm going now.'

'Bye!'

(These scripts can be made into prompt cards to use during play with peers.)

Resolving conflict

Situations that may cause conflict

- Taking a toy from another child.
- When asked to change an activity.
- Another's proximity.
- Disrupting other children's play.
- The child having to wait for his or her turn.
- Dominating the play.

Strategies to resolve conflict

- Adult intervenes calmly.
- Acknowledge the children's feelings.
- Gather information about what happened.
- Restate the problem.
- Ask for ideas about solutions.
- Support negotiations about how to go forward.

Social scripts for resolving conflict

- Hey! That's mine!
- I was using that!
- Let's share.
- Let's swap.
- Let's take turns.
- You can go first, then it's my turn.
- It's my turn now.
- Stop it!
- Don't do that!
- I don't want to play that.
- Let's play something else.
- I've got an idea!
- What do you want to do?

Adapted from: DfEE/QCA *Curriculum Guidance for the Foundation Stage*, May 2000

✓

Play a game with a friend

_____ ☺   and   _____ ☺

your name   your friend's name

We like to play:

Draw a picture of the game you like to play.

Ask your friend: 'Want to play?'

✓

Playing with a friend

Let's choose a game we both like

☺ I like _____

☺ You like _____

☹ I don't like _____

☹ You don't like _____

☺ + ☺ We both like _____

Let's play _____

Then we will both feel happy ☺ + ☺

Playing with friends

How to use the Let's Compromise! *sheet*

1. Offer a limited choice of games or toys (e.g. two to four) to begin with. Be sure to include a preferred game for each child.

2. Use the *Let's Compromise!* sheet to help the children organise their ideas and make their choices visually explicit.

3. The children fill in the first part of the sheet using pictures, symbols or words, or any combination. Stop at *Let's Compromise!*

4. Roll a dice to see whose game is played first. The highest scorer goes first. Complete the second part of the sheet (First… Then…).

5. Teach the children to wait until each player has finished his or her turn before taking their own (this is often a source of conflict). Use a 'Wait' card.

6. Teach the children what to say to winners (e.g. *Well played!*) and to losers (e.g. *Play another game?* or *Better luck next time!*). Write these phrases on cue cards to use as prompts.

7. Use a visual means (e.g. sand-timer, buzzer or clock) to count down the end of each activity and a visual schedule to show what happens next. These visual strategies help the children make the transition from one activity to another.

8. When the game has finished, there is often a tendency to walk off without reference to playmates. Use cue cards to prompt exit strategies – what to do and say when leaving peer play situations.

Playing with friends – Let's Compromise!

☺ I like to play _____

☺ You like to play _____

☺ + ☺ We like different games.

Let's compromise!

First let's play _____

Then let's play _____

Then we will both feel happy ☺ + ☺

Appendix 3
Small Steps Charts

Social Play Record

TYPE OF PLAY: EARLY SOCIAL PLAY (REACTIVE PLAY)

Key elements: Child reacts to adult who impinges on child's space.

SOCIAL PLAY BEHAVIOURS	RATING SCALE				COMMENTS	INTERVENTION	
	Often	Sometimes	When prompted	Rarely or never	Does context help or hinder? Look at situations, play partners, toys and materials, prompts.	Tick if required — Monitor item/s	Work on item/s
A. Reacts to people							
1. Startles	☐	☐	☐	☐			
2. Responds to familiar voices (e.g. stills/turns/smiles)	☐	☐	☐	☐			
3. Turns on hearing own name	☐	☐	☐	☐			
4. Looks at adult's face	☐	☐	☐	☐			
5. Smiles at others (with/without eye contact)	☐	☐	☐	☐			
6. Tolerates others' proximity	☐	☐	☐	☐			
7. Responds to touch, e.g. cuddles, tickles	☐	☐	☐	☐			
8. Responds to physical play (how?) e.g. lifting, rocking, bouncing, swinging	☐	☐	☐	☐			
9. Responds to repetitive social games e.g. Pounce! Tickle! Gone! *Ready, steady, go!* Chase and catch	☐	☐	☐	☐			

Social Play Record

TYPE OF PLAY: EARLY SOCIAL PLAY (REACTIVE PLAY)

SOCIAL PLAY BEHAVIOURS	RATING SCALE				COMMENTS	INTERVENTION	
	Often	Sometimes	When prompted	Rarely or never	Does context help or hinder? Look at situations, play partners, toys and materials, prompts.	Tick if required Monitor item/s	Work on item/s
B. Reacts to music							
1. Calms or stills to listen	☐	☐	☐	☐			
2. Moves body	☐	☐	☐	☐			
3. Vocalises	☐	☐	☐	☐			
4. Anticipates actions in action songs	☐	☐	☐	☐			
5. Joins in action songs non-verbally/verbally/both	☐	☐	☐	☐			
C. Joint attention							
1. Attends to objects presented (looks at/reaches for)	☐	☐	☐	☐			
2. Accepts objects offered	☐	☐	☐	☐			
3. Follows touch pointing	☐	☐	☐	☐			
4. Looks for hidden objects	☐	☐	☐	☐			
5. Plays peek-a-boo	☐	☐	☐	☐			
6. Follows distance pointing	☐	☐	☐	☐			

Name:

Date:

TYPE OF PLAY: EARLY SOCIAL PLAY (RECIPROCAL PLAY)

Key elements: Child takes more active part in the play. Joint activity, imitation, beginnings of turn-taking with carer.

SOCIAL PLAY BEHAVIOURS	RATING SCALE				COMMENTS	INTERVENTION	
	Often	Sometimes	When prompted	Rarely or never	Does context help or hinder? Look at situations, play partners, toys and materials, prompts.	Tick if required Monitor item/s	Work on item/s
A. Joint attention							
1. Gains adult's attention (how)?	☐	☐	☐	☐			
2. Alternates gaze between object and person	☐	☐	☐	☐			
3. Offers objects	☐	☐	☐	☐			
4. Brings/holds up objects to show	☐	☐	☐	☐			
5. Shares toys/books with adult	☐	☐	☐	☐			
6. Touch points (with/without intention to show?)	☐	☐	☐	☐			
7. Distance points (with/without intention to show?)	☐	☐	☐	☐			
8. Includes adults in his or her play	☐	☐	☐	☐			
B. Social referencing							
1. Observes adult's reactions	☐	☐	☐	☐			
2. Responds to or complements adult reactions	☐	☐	☐	☐			

Social Play Record

TYPE OF PLAY: EARLY SOCIAL PLAY (RECIPROCAL PLAY)

SOCIAL PLAY BEHAVIOURS	RATING SCALE				COMMENTS	INTERVENTION	
	Often	Sometimes	When prompted	Rarely or never	Does context help or hinder? Look at situations, play partners, toys and materials, prompts	Tick if required Monitor item/s	Work on item/s
C. Imitation							
1. Copies facial expression and gesture (e.g. smile, wave bye, shake/nod head)	☐	☐	☐	☐			
2. Copies actions with objects (e.g. bang, shake, blow, press, throw, push)	☐	☐	☐	☐			
3. Copies body movements (e.g. stretch, jump, wriggle, clap, stamp feet, wiggle fingers)	☐	☐	☐	☐			
4. Copies sounds (human/animal/vehicle)	☐	☐	☐	☐			
5. Reacts to being copied by adult and initiates activities for adult to copy	☐	☐	☐	☐			
D. Partner games							
1. Plays ball games with carer (e.g. rolling, kicking, throwing)	☐	☐	☐	☐			
2. Plays push/pull toys or games (e.g. wheeled or ride-on toys, tug-of-war)	☐	☐	☐	☐			

Name: Date:

Social Play Record

TYPE OF PLAY: INDEPENDENT PLAY (SOLITARY ACTIVITY)

Key elements: Plays alone and independently with toys different from those used by children within speaking distance. Pursues own activity without reference to others. Makes no effort to get close to other children.

SOCIAL PLAY BEHAVIOURS	RATING SCALE				COMMENTS	INTERVENTION	
	Often	Sometimes	When prompted	Rarely or never	Does context help or hinder? Look at situations, play partners, toys and materials, prompts.	Tick if required Monitor item/s	Work on item/s
A. Preoccupied activity							
1. Preoccupied with own body movements (e.g. flapping, spinning, rocking, flicking)	☐	☐	☐	☐			
2. Preoccupied with objects (specify)	☐	☐	☐	☐			
3. Preoccupied with actions (specify)	☐	☐	☐	☐			
4. Unusual manipulation of objects	☐	☐	☐	☐			
5. Resists attempts to stop or change activity	☐	☐	☐	☐			
6. Compulsion to complete tasks (e.g. puzzles, play routines)	☐	☐	☐	☐			
7. Appears unaware of others	☐	☐	☐	☐			
8. Talks to self (related/unrelated to context?)	☐	☐	☐	☐			
9. Response to others' attempts to join his or her activity: positive/negative/both?	☐	☐	☐	☐			

Social Play Record

TYPE OF PLAY: INDEPENDENT PLAY (SOLITARY ACTIVITY)

SOCIAL PLAY BEHAVIOURS	RATING SCALE			COMMENTS	INTERVENTION	
	Often	Sometimes	When prompted	Rarely or never	Does context help or hinder? Look at situations, play partners, toys and materials, prompts.	Tick if required Monitor item/s	Work on item/s

B. Functional play

SOCIAL PLAY BEHAVIOURS	Often	Sometimes	When prompted	Rarely or never	COMMENTS	Monitor item/s	Work on item/s
1. Explores objects (e.g. touches, mouths)	☐	☐	☐	☐			
2. Performs actions on objects (e.g. bangs, shakes, pulls, pushes, throws, empties, fills, posts)	☐	☐	☐	☐			
3. Operates cause/effect toys (e.g. pushes buttons, works switches, turns dials)	☐	☐	☐	☐			
4. Performs motor activities (e.g. running, jumping, twirling)	☐	☐	☐	☐			
5. Plays with real objects (e.g. cup, spoon, brush) according to their function	☐	☐	☐	☐			
6. Plays with reality-based toys (e.g. pushes car or train along, hugs doll, puts toy phone to ear)	☐	☐	☐	☐			
7. Combines objects or toys in play (e.g. feeds doll, hat on teddy, car in garage, bricks on truck)	☐	☐	☐	☐			
8. Plays with miniature reality-based toys (e.g. animals, play people)	☐	☐	☐	☐			
9. Chooses activities appropriate to the situation (e.g. ball for outdoor play)	☐	☐	☐	☐			
10. Exhibits a range of play activities rather than repetitive play	☐	☐	☐	☐			

Name:

Date:

Social Play Record

TYPE OF PLAY: INDEPENDENT PLAY (SOLITARY ACTIVITY)

SOCIAL PLAY BEHAVIOURS	RATING SCALE				COMMENTS	INTERVENTION	
	Often	Sometimes	When prompted	Rarely or never	Does context help or hinder? Look at situations, play partners, toys and materials, prompts.	Tick if required Monitor item/s	Work on item/s
C. Constructional play							
1. Uses materials to construct (e.g. bricks, Lego, Duplo)	☐	☐	☐	☐			
2. Uses materials to create (e.g. sand, plasticine, 'junk')	☐	☐	☐	☐			
D. Self-pretend play							
1. Pretends actions (e.g. sleeping, brushing hair, driving, cooking, drinking)	☐	☐	☐	☐			
2. Pretends emotions (specify)	☐	☐	☐	☐			
3. Pretends characters (specify): familiar, fictional or fantasy?	☐	☐	☐	☐			
E. Object pretend play							
1. Play includes gestures, sound effects, vocalisation or speech (specify)	☐	☐	☐	☐			
2. Attributes properties, feelings or beliefs to toys (e.g. makes doll 'cry', washes 'dirty' car)	☐	☐	☐	☐			
3. Substitutes objects similar in shape or function (e.g. box for garage)	☐	☐	☐	☐			
4. Substitutes objects dissimilar in shape or function (e.g. brick for car)	☐	☐	☐	☐			
5. Uses non-representational materials in inventive ways (e.g. 'junk' play)	☐	☐	☐	☐			
6. Creates imaginary objects to support play	☐	☐	☐	☐			

Social Play Record

TYPE OF PLAY: INDEPENDENT PLAY (SOLITARY ACTIVITY)

SOCIAL PLAY BEHAVIOURS	RATING SCALE				COMMENTS	INTERVENTION	
	Often	Sometimes	When prompted	Rarely or never	Does context help or hinder? Look at situations, play partners, toys and materials, prompts.	Tick if required Monitor item/s	Work on item/s
F. Sequenced pretend play							
1. Carries out familiar pretend actions in related sequence – circle: familiar/fictional/fantasy (e.g. preparing and eating food, getting ready for bed/school, acting out stories from films/TV/video)	☐	☐	☐	☐			
2. Carries out sequence repeatedly with little variation	☐	☐	☐	☐			
3. Role play (familiar/fictional/fantasy?):	☐	☐	☐	☐			
• plays the role of another							
• gives toys a role							
• engages in elaborate 'small world' play with miniatures							
• shows empathy within roles (feelings, desires, beliefs)							
• creates own imaginative roles							
G. Interests/hobbies							
1. Spends most of free time engaged in own particular interest or hobby	☐	☐	☐	☐			
H. Flexible thinking							
1. Differentiates pretence from real	☐	☐	☐	☐			
2. Plays with ideas	☐	☐	☐	☐			
3. Produces creative writing or art	☐	☐	☐	☐			

Name: Date:

Social Play Record

TYPE OF PLAY: PEER PLAY – EXTENT OF SOCIAL PARTICIPATION

TYPE OF PEER PLAY	DESCRIPTION	RATING SCALE				KEY INTERVENTION STRATEGIES
		Often	Sometimes	When prompted	Rarely or never	
Observer	Child is a spectator. Passive observation without actual participation.	☐	☐	☐	☐	• Work on parallel play. • Teach imitation. • Work on proximity.
Parallel	Child plays *beside* rather than with others, within the same physical space but independently. Child plays with toys/materials similar to those around him or her and *imitates* others, but maintains independent play.	☐	☐	☐	☐	• Work on entry skills. • Work on maintenance skills.
Associative	Plays *with* other children *sharing materials*, but play is still independent, each child playing as he or she wishes. The activity may be similar or identical but is not organised around any mutual activity or goal. Awareness of others develops.	☐	☐	☐	☐	• Work on maintenance skills. • Check cognitive levels of play.
Co-operative	Play is *co-ordinated* with and *complements* others' play. Sharing of attention, materials and activities, taking turns. Common goals and complementary roles.	☐	☐	☐	☐	• Check strategies for avoiding or resolving conflict. • Work on socio-dramatic play. • Work on exit strategies.

Social Play Record

TYPE OF PLAY: PEER PLAY – COGNITIVE SOPHISTICATION

COGNITIVE LEVEL OF PLAY Play with others involves	RATING SCALE				COMMENTS Does context help or hinder? Look at situations, play partners, toys and materials, prompts.
	Often	Sometimes	When prompted	Rarely or never	
Physical or **sensory play** (e.g. visual or tactile exploration, running, climbing, swinging)	☐	☐	☐	☐	
Functional play (using large and small world toys)	☐	☐	☐	☐	
Constructional play (e.g. bricks, Lego, sand)	☐	☐	☐	☐	
Board games (e.g. picture lotto, snakes and ladders)	☐	☐	☐	☐	
Pretend play (e.g. pretend objects or feelings, imaginative use of toys/materials)	☐	☐	☐	☐	
Role play (e.g. familiar or imaginative themes, with or without dressing-up clothes/props)	☐	☐	☐	☐	
Team games	☐	☐	☐	☐	

Name:

Date:

SOCIAL PLAY RECORD

TYPE OF PLAY: PEER PLAY – OBSERVER

SOCIAL PLAY BEHAVIOURS	RATING SCALE				COMMENTS	INTERVENTION	
	Often	Sometimes	When prompted	Rarely or never	Does context help or hinder? Look at situations, play partners, toys and materials, prompts.	Tick if required Monitor item/s	Work on item/s
1. Watches peers without attempting to join in	☐	☐	☐	☐			
2. Comments on peers' activities	☐	☐	☐	☐			
3. Copies those he or she is watching	☐	☐	☐	☐			
4. Sits or stands within speaking distance	☐	☐	☐	☐			
5. Orientates body towards peers	☐	☐	☐	☐			
6. Gestures, vocalises or speaks to those he or she is watching	☐	☐	☐	☐			
7. Responds to others' approaches (describe how)	☐	☐	☐	☐			

Social Play Record

TYPE OF PLAY: PEER PLAY – PARALLEL PLAY

Key elements: Child plays beside rather than with others, within the same physical space but independently.
Child plays with toys/materials similar to those around him or her and *imitates* others, but maintains independent play.

SOCIAL PLAY BEHAVIOURS	RATING SCALE				COMMENTS	INTERVENTION	
	Often	Sometimes	When prompted	Rarely or never	Does context help or hinder? Look at situations, play partners, toys and materials, prompts.	Tick if required Monitor item/s	Work on item/s
A. Timing							
1. Imitation is immediate	☐	☐	☐	☐			
2. Imitation is delayed	☐	☐	☐	☐			
B. Appropriacy							
1. Imitation is appropriate	☐	☐	☐	☐			
2. Imitation is unusual/atypical	☐	☐	☐	☐			
C. Social awareness							
1. Child comments on activity	☐	☐	☐	☐			
2. Child looks at those he or she is copying	☐	☐	☐	☐			
3. Child speaks to those he or she is copying	☐	☐	☐	☐			
D. Type of play copied							
1. Functional play (through actions, sounds or speech)	☐	☐	☐	☐			
2. Constructional play (e.g. bricks, models)	☐	☐	☐	☐			
3. Pretend play	☐	☐	☐	☐			
4. Role play	☐	☐	☐	☐			

Name: Date:

Social Play Record

TYPE OF PLAY: PEER PLAY – ENTRY SKILLS

SOCIAL PLAY BEHAVIOURS	RATING SCALE				COMMENTS	INTERVENTION	
	Often	Sometimes	When prompted	Rarely or never	Does context help or hinder? Look at situations, play partners, toys and materials, prompts.	Tick if required	
						Monitor item/s	Work on item/s
A. Response to peers							
1. Stands/sits near peers	☐	☐	☐	☐			
2. Imitates peers	☐	☐	☐	☐			
3. Smiles at peers	☐	☐	☐	☐			
4. Greets peers by name	☐	☐	☐	☐			
5. Speaks to peer/s (comments on the activity, asks to play)	☐	☐	☐	☐			
6. Offers toy/materials	☐	☐	☐	☐			
7. Accepts toy/materials	☐	☐	☐	☐			
8. Allows peers to join his or her activities	☐	☐	☐	☐			
9. Invites peers to join his or her activities	☐	☐	☐	☐			
10. States intention to join in	☐	☐	☐	☐			
11. Suggests role for self	☐	☐	☐	☐			
12. Attempts to initiate play in unusual or inappropriate ways (e.g. pushes or hits others, takes/snatches/throws toys)	☐	☐	☐	☐			

Social Play Record

TYPE OF PLAY: PEER PLAY – ENTRY SKILLS

SOCIAL PLAY BEHAVIOURS	RATING SCALE				COMMENTS	INTERVENTION	
	Often	Sometimes	When prompted	Rarely or never	Does context help or hinder? Look at situations, play partners, toys and materials, prompts.	Tick if required Monitor item/s	Work on item/s
B. Invitations to play							
1. Is invited to join others' play	☐	☐	☐	☐			
2. Accepts appropriately	☐	☐	☐	☐			
3. Refuses appropriately	☐	☐	☐	☐			
C. Ease of entry into peer play							
1. Successful entry	☐	☐	☐	☐			
2. Inept entry skills	☐	☐	☐	☐			
3. Attempts are rejected or ignored	☐	☐	☐	☐			

Name:

Date:

TYPE OF PLAY: PEER PLAY – MAINTENANCE SKILLS

SOCIAL PLAY BEHAVIOURS	RATING SCALE				COMMENTS	INTERVENTION	
	Often	Sometimes	When prompted	Rarely or never	Does context help or hinder? Look at situations, play partners, toys and materials, prompts.	Tick if required Monitor item/s	Work on item/s
A. Activities to maintain peer play							
1. Follows peers around	☐	☐	☐	☐			
2. Plays at appropriate distance	☐	☐	☐	☐			
3. Parallel activity develops into mutual game	☐	☐	☐	☐			
4. Shares/exchanges materials	☐	☐	☐	☐			
5. Takes turns	☐	☐	☐	☐			
6. Waits for others to finish their turn	☐	☐	☐	☐			
7. Talks about the activity	☐	☐	☐	☐			
8. Offers suggestions	☐	☐	☐	☐			
9. Accepts others' suggestions	☐	☐	☐	☐			
10. Inhibits rituals and stereotypes	☐	☐	☐	☐			
11. Shares positive affect (e.g. smiles/laughs with peers)	☐	☐	☐	☐			
12. Sustains play with peers for several minutes	☐	☐	☐	☐			

Social Play Record

TYPE OF PLAY: PEER PLAY – MAINTENANCE SKILLS

SOCIAL PLAY BEHAVIOURS	RATING SCALE				COMMENTS	INTERVENTION	
	Often	Sometimes	When prompted	Rarely or never	Does context help or hinder? Look at situations, play partners, toys and materials, prompts.	Tick if required Monitor item/s	Work on item/s
B. Flexibility of play							
1. Copes with changes of activity	☐	☐	☐	☐			
2. Uses toys/materials flexibly	☐	☐	☐	☐			
3. Chooses activities appropriate to the context	☐	☐	☐	☐			
C. Attempts to control play							
1. Participates in planning/choosing/deciding	☐	☐	☐	☐			
2. Takes over/dominates activities	☐	☐	☐	☐			
3. Censors who does/does not join	☐	☐	☐	☐			
4. Sets the rules/rigidly applies rules	☐	☐	☐	☐			
D. Empathy							
1. Empathises with others' needs	☐	☐	☐	☐			
2. Empathises with others' feelings	☐	☐	☐	☐			
3. Supports others	☐	☐	☐	☐			
4. Consults others	☐	☐	☐	☐			
5. Anticipates consequences of actions and decisions	☐	☐	☐	☐			

Name: Date:

TYPE OF PLAY: PEER PLAY – MAINTENANCE SKILLS

SOCIAL PLAY BEHAVIOURS	RATING SCALE				COMMENTS	INTERVENTION	
	Often	Sometimes	When prompted	Rarely or never	Does context help or hinder? Look at situations, play partners, toys and materials, prompts.	Tick if required Monitor item/s	Work on item/s
E. Humour							
1. Teases others	☐	☐	☐	☐			
2. Knows when to stop teasing	☐	☐	☐	☐			
3. Copes with being teased	☐	☐	☐	☐			
4. Jokes: laughs at the right time	☐	☐	☐	☐			
5. Attempts to tells jokes	☐	☐	☐	☐			
F. Disagreement, conflict and confrontation							
1. Knows when he or she has upset or annoyed others	☐	☐	☐	☐			
2. Apologises for upsetting or annoying others	☐	☐	☐	☐			
3. Persists in upsetting or annoying others	☐	☐	☐	☐			
4. Accepts apology from others	☐	☐	☐	☐			
5. Is susceptible to bullying	☐	☐	☐	☐			
6. Tells tales	☐	☐	☐	☐			
7. Seeks adult's help appropriately	☐	☐	☐	☐			
8. Suggests a compromise (e.g. sharing, exchanging, taking turns)	☐	☐	☐	☐			

Social Play Record

TYPE OF PLAY: PEER PLAY – EXIT SKILLS

SOCIAL PLAY BEHAVIOURS	RATING SCALE				COMMENTS	INTERVENTION	
	Often	Sometimes	When prompted	Rarely or never	Does context help or hinder? Look at situations, play partners, toys and materials, prompts.	Tick if required **Monitor item/s**	**Work on item/s**
A. Exit Skills							
1. Tells peers when he or she wants to do something else	☐	☐	☐	☐			
2. Tells peers he or she has finished playing, using gesture or speech (e.g. 'I'm off now!')	☐	☐	☐	☐			
3. Leaves at appropriate moment	☐	☐	☐	☐			
4. Any other strategies (specify)	☐	☐	☐	☐			
5. Leaves activities without reference to peers	☐	☐	☐	☐			

Name:

Date:

TYPE OF PLAY: ADVANCED GROUP SKILLS

Key elements: More sophisticated group skills emerge, such as group identity and roles, use of compromise, negotiation and persuasion, competition.

SOCIAL PLAY BEHAVIOURS	RATING SCALE				COMMENTS	INTERVENTION	
	Often	Sometimes	When prompted	Rarely or never	Does context help or hinder? Look at situations, play partners, toys and materials, prompts.	Tick if required Monitor item/s	Work on item/s
A. Advanced entry skills							
1. Watches peers whilst gradually approaching group	☐	☐	☐	☐			
2. Hovers on periphery	☐	☐	☐	☐			
3. Imitates peers	☐	☐	☐	☐			
4. Comments on group's activity	☐	☐	☐	☐			
5. Gradually moves closer	☐	☐	☐	☐			
6. Waits for an invitation or natural break without disrupting the group's activity	☐	☐	☐	☐			
B. Group identity							
1. Has a sense of belonging to a group	☐	☐	☐	☐			
2. Follows the group's interests	☐	☐	☐	☐			
C. Conforms to group norms							
1. Behaviour	☐	☐	☐	☐			
2. Activities	☐	☐	☐	☐			
3. Speech	☐	☐	☐	☐			
4. Attitudes	☐	☐	☐	☐			
5. Dress	☐	☐	☐	☐			

Social Play Record

TYPE OF PLAY: ADVANCED GROUP SKILLS

SOCIAL PLAY BEHAVIOURS	RATING SCALE				COMMENTS	INTERVENTION	
	Often	Sometimes	When prompted	Rarely or never	Does context help or hinder? Look at situations, play partners, toys and materials, prompts.	Tick if required Monitor item/s	Work on item/s
D. Group role and participation							
1. Easily led/taken advantage of	☐	☐	☐	☐			
2. Knows how to lead	☐	☐	☐	☐			
3. Knows when to follow	☐	☐	☐	☐			
4. Contributes to planning	☐	☐	☐	☐			
5. Participates in preparation	☐	☐	☐	☐			
6. Supports others in roles	☐	☐	☐	☐			
E. Rules							
1. Applies rules appropriately	☐	☐	☐	☐			
2. Adapts rules	☐	☐	☐	☐			
F. Disagreement, conflict and confrontation							
1. Appreciates another's viewpoint	☐	☐	☐	☐			
2. Uses compromise strategies (e.g. shares, exchanges, takes turns)	☐	☐	☐	☐			
3. Uses negotiation or persuasion (e.g. bargains, trades, bribes)	☐	☐	☐	☐			
4. Attempts reconciliation (offers apology to make amends)	☐	☐	☐	☐			
5. Asserts views/rights	☐	☐	☐	☐			

Name: Date:

Social Play Record

TYPE OF PLAY: ADVANCED GROUP SKILLS

SOCIAL PLAY BEHAVIOURS	RATING SCALE				COMMENTS	INTERVENTION	
	Often	Sometimes	When prompted	Rarely or never	Does context help or hinder? Look at situations, play partners, toys and materials, prompts.	Tick if required Monitor item/s	Work on item/s
G. Complaining							
1. Complains appropriately	☐	☐	☐	☐			
2. Dwells on real or imagined wrongs	☐	☐	☐	☐			
3. Complains about rule breaking	☐	☐	☐	☐			
H. Competition/team games							
1. Shows interest in team games and competitive sports	☐	☐	☐	☐			
2. Participates as a team member	☐	☐	☐	☐			
3. Copes with winning	☐	☐	☐	☐			
4. Copes with losing	☐	☐	☐	☐			
5. Makes competitive statements	☐	☐	☐	☐			
6. Has a sense of fair play	☐	☐	☐	☐			

Social Play Record

TYPE OF PLAY: FRIENDSHIP SKILLS

Key elements: Acceptance and rejection of and by peers. Understanding of friendship develops. Formation and maintenance of friendships.

SOCIAL PLAY BEHAVIOURS	RATING SCALE				COMMENTS	INTERVENTION	
	Often	Sometimes	When prompted	Rarely or never	Does context help or hinder? Look at situations, play partners, toys and materials, prompts.	Tick if required Monitor item/s	Work on item/s
A. Rejection of peers Specify how:							
1. Ignores or avoids	☐	☐	☐	☐			
2. Rejects non-verbally or verbally	☐	☐	☐	☐			
3. Gives reason for rejection	☐	☐	☐	☐			
B. Rejection by peers							
1. Recognises rejection	☐	☐	☐	☐			
2. Becomes upset	☐	☐	☐	☐			
3. Becomes angry	☐	☐	☐	☐			
4. Tries again	☐	☐	☐	☐			
5. Accepts rejection	☐	☐	☐	☐			
6. Understands reason for rejection	☐	☐	☐	☐			
7. Approaches another peer	☐	☐	☐	☐			

Name: Date:

TYPE OF PLAY: FRIENDSHIP SKILLS

SOCIAL PLAY BEHAVIOURS	RATING SCALE				COMMENTS	INTERVENTION	
	Often	Sometimes	When prompted	Rarely or never	Does context help or hinder? Look at situations, play partners, toys and materials, prompts.	Tick if required Monitor item/s	Work on item/s
C. Making friends							
1. Is motivated to socialise (desires to interact, have friends, fit in)	☐	☐	☐	☐			
2. Interacts with peers in preference to adults	☐	☐	☐	☐			
3. Is accepted by peers	☐	☐	☐	☐			
4. Has preferred playmates	☐	☐	☐	☐			
5. Chooses age-appropriate peers	☐	☐	☐	☐			
6. Invites peers to play/do things	☐	☐	☐	☐			
7. Asks to join peers	☐	☐	☐	☐			
8. Accepts invitations from peers	☐	☐	☐	☐			
9. Differentiates friends from playmateS (by more positive and fewer negative behaviours)	☐	☐	☐	☐			
10. Has a reciprocated friendship (laughs and smiles with friend, spends 30% time or more with, maintains proximity within 3 ft)	☐	☐	☐	☐			
11. Has more than one mutual friend	☐	☐	☐	☐			
12. Uses friendship status as a means of group entry	☐	☐	☐	☐			

Social Play Record

TYPE OF PLAY: FRIENDSHIP SKILLS

SOCIAL PLAY BEHAVIOURS	RATING SCALE				COMMENTS	INTERVENTION	
	Often	Sometimes	When prompted	Rarely or never	Does context help or hinder? Look at situations, play partners, toys and materials, prompts.	Tick if required Monitor item/s	Work on item/s
D. Sustaining friendships							
1. Greets friends	☐	☐	☐	☐			
2. Plays with friends	☐	☐	☐	☐			
3. Is fun to be with	☐	☐	☐	☐			
4. Offers practical support (lends items, shares materials, helps friends, defends friends)	☐	☐	☐	☐			
5. Seeks help from friends (practical assistance, advice)	☐	☐	☐	☐			
6. Invites friends to house or party	☐	☐	☐	☐			
7. Receives invitations to friend's house or party	☐	☐	☐	☐			
8. Talks about own likes, interests and opinions	☐	☐	☐	☐			
9. Finds out about friend's likes, interests and opinions	☐	☐	☐	☐			
10. Shares own interests and activities	☐	☐	☐	☐			
11. Accommodates friend's interests and activities	☐	☐	☐	☐			
12. Knows when and how to apologise	☐	☐	☐	☐			
13. Knows when and how to thank	☐	☐	☐	☐			
14. Knows how to pay and receive compliments	☐	☐	☐	☐			
15. Knows how to give and take criticism	☐	☐	☐	☐			

Name: Date:

Social Play Record

TYPE OF PLAY: FRIENDSHIP SKILLS

SOCIAL PLAY BEHAVIOURS	RATING SCALE				COMMENTS	INTERVENTION	
	Often	Sometimes	When prompted	Rarely or never	Does context help or hinder? Look at situations, play partners, toys and materials, prompts.	Tick if required Monitor item/s	Work on item/s
E. Interactional style							
1. Relies on ritual and routine to interact with peers	☐	☐	☐	☐			
2. Uses speech and/or gesture	☐	☐	☐	☐			
3. Invites/suggests/requests	☐	☐	☐	☐			
4. Demands/dictates/controls	☐	☐	☐	☐			
5. Level of familiarity is appropriate	☐	☐	☐	☐			
F. Conversational skills							
1. Stands at appropriate distance	☐	☐	☐	☐			
2. Knows when to join in	☐	☐	☐	☐			
3. Knows how to join in	☐	☐	☐	☐			
4. Talks to, not at others	☐	☐	☐	☐			
5. Gives listener feedback (eye contact, nods, appropriate comments)	☐	☐	☐	☐			
6. Acts on listener feedback (e.g. notes disinterest/desire to speak)	☐	☐	☐	☐			
7. Takes conversational turns	☐	☐	☐	☐			
8. Times turns appropriately	☐	☐	☐	☐			
9. Maintains topic of conversation using relevant comments/questions	☐	☐	☐	☐			
10. Shares information	☐	☐	☐	☐			
11. Changes topic appropriately	☐	☐	☐	☐			
12. Ends conversation appropriately	☐	☐	☐	☐			

Social Play Record

TYPE OF PLAY: FRIENDSHIP SKILLS

SOCIAL PLAY BEHAVIOURS	RATING SCALE				COMMENTS	INTERVENTION	
	Often	Sometimes	When prompted	Rarely or never	Does context help or hinder? Look at situations, play partners, toys and materials, prompts.	Tick if required Monito item/s	Work on item/s
G. Social and emotional reciprocity							
1. Shares positive affect with friends (smiles/laughs)	□	□	□	□			
2. Recognises feelings of friends	□	□	□	□			
3. Shows concern for friends if they are hurt or upset	□	□	□	□			
4. Expresses own feelings appropriately	□	□	□	□			
5. Is aware of how own behaviour affects others	□	□	□	□			
6. Seeks to make amends	□	□	□	□			
7. Confides feelings	□	□	□	□			
8. Shares experiences	□	□	□	□			
9. Shares secrets with friends	□	□	□	□			
10. Shares humour	□	□	□	□			
11. Exchanges friendly teasing	□	□	□	□			
12. Respects differences	□	□	□	□			
H. Self-perception of social effectiveness							
1. Unaware	□	□	□	□			
2. Negative perception	□	□	□	□			
3. Positive perception	□	□	□	□			

Name: Date:

Appendix 4
Theory and Research

The development of social play

What is social play?

Social play is play with others. It is a deceptively simple term. Social play is a lifelong learning process, critical to social competence (Arthur, Bochner and Butterfield, 1999), a primary social and cultural activity for acquiring symbolic capacity, interpersonal skills and social knowledge (Vygotsky, 1978) and a useful indicator of developmental progress (Moyles, 1994). Research has consistently shown that social play and friendships are important for linguistic, cognitive, socio-emotional and cultural development and for physical and mental health, long-term adjustment and quality of life (Alvarez, Reid and Hodges, 1999; Howlin, Marwood and Rutter, 2000; Rubin, 2002; Sigman and McGovern, 2005; Siller and Sigman, 2002). Social play is also being linked to wider social and economic objectives, as the contribution play can make to reducing crime and antisocial behaviour is increasingly recognised (Department of Media, Culture and Sport, 2004).

Social play is not a linear process involving a discrete set of skills. It is complex, dynamic, culturally influenced and contextually based (Strain and Schwartz, 2001). Three dimensions are fundamental to its development: first, *social processes* (shared attention understanding and emotional regulation) which underlie social competence (Guralnick, 1993); second, the *complexity of cognitive play* as expansion in cognitive activities fosters longer and more complex interaction (Malone and Langone, 1999; Williams, Reddy and Costall, 2001); third, *social status*, that is evaluation of and by others (Hepler, 1997; Howes, 1996). A combination of skill, opportunity and experience is considered essential for children at all stages of social play (Hurley-Geffner, 1995; Wolfberg, 2005).

Social play begins as interactive, interpersonal exchanges between infant and caregiver, develops into increasingly sophisticated social functioning with peers and peer groups and extends into the formation of friendships, meaningful relationships and social networks. Pivotal developmental markers are identifiable within each stage. Early interactional play develops the prosocial skills of interpersonal engagement, joint attention, imitation of and by others and social routines (Carpenter, Pennington and Rogers, 2002; Charman *et al.*, 2000). These processes are fundamental to later social and linguistic competence, fostering interpersonal awareness, synchronisation and emotional referencing

(Hobson, 1993; Jones and Carr, 2004; Mundy and Crowson, 1997; Sigman and McGovern, 2005; Siller and Sigman, 2002; Trevarthen and Aitken, 2001).

Responsiveness to others and reciprocity in interactions continue to be important for peer play and friendship formation (Howes, 1987; Travis, Sigman and Ruskin, 2001; Wolfberg, 2005). Essential processes for successful peer play include entry, maintenance and exit strategies (Guralnick, 1993; Wolfberg, 1995). The degree to which children are motivated to socialise and adapt to changing social demands are also significant factors (Guralnick and Neville, 1997; Malone, 1999). Key skills include: observing others; gaining peers' attention; signalling interest in activities and imitating; playing in physical proximity; sharing and taking turns; conflict resolution and emotional control (Stevahn *et al.*, 2000). Pretend play, particularly sociodramatic role play, and linguistic competence assume increasing importance for peer interaction in order to sustain and extend activities (Howes and Matheson, 1992; Schuler, 2003; Schuler and Wolfberg, 1999).

Critical markers for advanced group play include more sophisticated entry strategies, peer group identity, managing emotions, coping with disagreement, handling rejection/refusal, flexible application of rules and team skills (Nesdale and Flesser, 2001). These depend on increasingly sophisticated social understanding and social communication. Social status becomes crucial at this stage (DiSalvo and Oswald, 2002; Hepler, 1997). Then, as more time is spent with peers, the focus transfers to friendships which not only require but also facilitate social skills (Bauminger and Shulman, 2003). Friendships offer numerous benefits, including emotional support, entry into and acceptance by peer groups and protection from teasing and bullying (Frea, 1995; Jordan and Jones, 1999). The purposes, dimensions, developmental progression, facilitation and maintenance of friendship have been identified as important factors (Bauminger and Kasari, 2001; Howes, 1987, 1996; Hurley-Geffner, 1995). Key developmental markers are shared interests or abilities, a positive affective style, flexible social interaction, humour, social empathy, mutual support and, at later stages, shared values and self-disclosure (Attwood, 1998; Hartrup, 1992; Rubin, 2002).

Social play and children with autistic spectrum disorders

> It is not that children with autism don't play – they do, in their own particular ways. (Boucher 1999, p.1)

A review by Trevarthen *et al.* (1996) concluded that although many kinds of play are less affected in children with autistic spectrum disorders than is generally supposed, social participation is the one dimension of play that consistently differentiates these children from their routinely developing peers. Social play involves increasing levels of cognition, communication and co-operation, and children with ASDs experience most difficulty when required to integrate cognitive with social activity. Not surprisingly then, social play, especially peer interaction, is a key diagnostic indicator (American Psychiatric Association, 1994).

Qualitative and quantitative differences are consistently reported in the social play of children with autistic spectrum disorders. Differences affect social complexity, cognitive diversity and social status, the three dimensions critical to the development of social play. Lack of spontaneous engagement in early social play is commonly described, with few initiations, infrequent sharing of attention, little emotional referencing or reciprocity (Charman, 1998; Jones and Carr, 2004; Sigman, 1998; Stahl and Pry, 2002; Wimpory *et al.*, 2000) and abnormally delayed and atypical imitation (Malvy *et al.*, 1999; Receveur *et al.*, 2005; Rogers, 1998; Williams, Whiten and Singh, 2004). Lack of spontaneous engagement in peer play is also consistently described, with lower rates of observer behaviour, initiation and responsivity to social bids (Jackson *et al.*, 2003; Lord and Magill, 1989; Lord and Magill-Evans, 1995; Wolfberg, 2005; Zanolli, Daggett and Adams, 1996). The children spend more time unoccupied or in solitary play, often absorbed in manipulative and ritualistic activity (Brown and Whiten, 2000; Frith, 1989; Howlin, 1998). Limitations in social communication cause difficulty understanding others' intentions and feelings, sharing perspectives, exchanging ideas, and playing co-operatively (Barratt *et al.*, 2000; Lawson, 2001; Weitzman, 1992). Studies suggest that individuals with autism make few personal friendships and have limited social participation (Attwood, 1998; Bauminger and Shulman, 2003; Orsmond, Krauss and Seltzer, 2004). Difficulties with reciprocity, emotional control, humour, empathy and experience sharing restrict the development of friendships, thus increasing the likelihood of social isolation (Gutstein and Whitney, 2002; Howlin, Baron-Cohen and Hadwin, 1999; Sainsbury, 2000). Specific help is usually needed to establish and maintain friendships.

Widespread differences are reported in object play, which typically features solitary, repetitive, manipulatory or self-stimulatory activities (Beyer and Gammeltoft 2000; Williams *et al.*, 2001; van Berckelaer-Onnes, 2003). Less functional, varied and interpersonal object play impacts on the development of social play, as shared understanding/use of objects plays a key role in facilitating interaction (Ingersoll, Schreibman and Tran, 2003; Malone and Langone, 1999; Williams, 2003; Williams, Costall and Reddy, 1999). Difficulties with the symbolic dimensions of play are consistently described, the children rarely producing spontaneous or novel acts of pretence in free play (Jarrold, Boucher and Smith, 1993; Roeyers and van Berckelaer-Onnes, 1994; Rutherford and Rogers, 2003; Wolfberg, 1995). This restricts opportunities for developing social play, which is extended through imaginative play with peers (Howes and Matheson, 1992; Wolfberg, 1999). Structured and elicited pretend play is reportedly less impaired (Charman and Baron-Cohen, 1997; Jarrold, 2003), offering avenues for intervention (Howlin *et al.*, 1999; Schuler, 2003; Sherratt and Peter, 2002).

Social play subsumes a range of processes and skills within the domains of social understanding and communication, social interaction and relationships, imagination and flexibility of thought and behaviour (Beyer and Gammeltoft, 2000). Children with autistic spectrum disorders have complex needs in these areas, so are likely to face significant challenges in acquiring social play skills. Given the intrinsic and pervasive nature of these difficulties, practitioners may well question the validity of intervention. Strong arguments have been put forward for developing social play. First, as already mentioned, research has consistently linked social play and friendships to development and learning, physical and mental health, long-term adjustment and quality of life. Second, practitioners should consider the issue of meaningful choice. The United Nations *Declaration of the Rights of the Child* (1959) states that all children have a basic right to full participation in their peer play culture. Wolfberg (1999) argues that this is an important ethical consideration for children with ASDs. But, as Attwood (1998) suggests, the children vary in the extent to which they want to socialise and make friends. Practitioners must determine whether apparent preference for social isolation represents a meaningful choice or if it arises from fear, inexperience or lack of skills (Williams, 1992, 1996).

A third argument is that difficulties in social play and friendship formation are a barrier to children's ability to learn and to achieve, reducing the potential benefits of inclusive environments (Guldberg, 2001; Mesibov and Shea, 1996). Problems with social play highlight children's differences from others. Inappropriate responses to the social advances of peers, unorthodox approaches and unusual play preferences often exclude children with ASDs from social play (Wolfberg and Schuler, 1999). Peer groups commonly tease, exploit or reject the children and may overwhelm their sensory tolerance, causing retreat (Sainsbury, 2000). Research has shown that solitary children and those who are perceived as 'different' are significantly more vulnerable to intimidation and bullying (Gray, 2002). These difficulties may cause parents increasingly to withdraw from social activities, restricting family life and limiting opportunities for social integration within the community, thereby intensifying the children's isolation (Jordan and Jones, 1999).

Whilst regular contact with typically developing peers provides valuable learning experiences, inclusion alone is unlikely to develop the requisite skills or processes of social play (Anderson *et al.*, 2004; Bauminger *et al.*, 2003; Gutstein and Sheely, 2002; Howlin, 1998; Zercher *et al.*, 2001). Without some form of skilled intervention, children with ASDs risk leading impoverished lives, with absence of social play perpetuating a cycle of exclusion, lack of experience and isolation. This deprives the children of critical opportunities for developing 'skill in understanding other people that is so necessary for integration into social life'. (Wing, 1996, p.25). Well-targeted intervention based on comprehensive assessment is required, combined with opportunity and experience (Attwood, 2000; Boucher, 1999; Jordan and Libby, 1997; McConnell, 2002). A growing number of outcome studies show that when appropriate intervention is provided, children with ASDs can and do make qualitative and quantitative gains in the competency of their social play (Bauminger, 2002; Bernard-Opitz, Ing and Kong, 2004; Dawson and Osterling, 1997; Jordan, 2003; Jordan, Jones and Murray, 1998; Odom *et al.*, 2003; Rogers, 2000; Strain and Schwartz, 2001; Wolfberg and Schuler, 1999).

How the Social Play Record was developed

The Social Play Record was developed by the author in collaboration with parents, teachers, learning support assistants, speech and language therapists and children with autistic spectrum disorders. It evolved through a combination of firsthand experience, collaborative projects, field trials and literature study to identify key factors in the development and assessment of social play in children with and without autistic spectrum disorders. The idea originated through concern that, despite opportunities to mix with sociable peers, many of our children with ASDs were making least year-on-year progress in social play compared to other areas of social interaction. The literature confirmed our observation that experience, whilst necessary, is not sufficient in itself. Children who are socially isolated cannot learn complex social skills simply by being placed with sociable children (Gutstein and Sheely, 2002; Kunce and Mesibov, 1998; Lord, 1995).

A further consideration was the interdependence of play and communication (Corke, 2002; Lewis, 2003). Through social play, children develop the skills of interpersonal engagement through which communication develops and competency with language improves (Chandler *et al.*, 2002; Guralnick *et al.*, 1996; Trevarthen *et al.*, 1996). However, our children were experiencing difficulty using play as a vehicle for learning. This created a dual dilemma: it precluded the therapeutic use of play to develop communication skills and restricted access to social contexts for the development of communicative competence. It was apparent that for children with autistic spectrum disorders social play must become the goal rather than the vehicle of intervention.

A comprehensive review of well-substantiated literature, from Parten's seminal work in 1932 to current work, showed that social play, particularly that of children with autistic spectrum disorders, has been and continues to be well researched. The literature emphasised the need for specific assessment measures in order to provide a focused framework for targeting intervention, with planning based on carefully collected evidence of skills and needs (Cumine, Leach and Stevenson, 2000; Guralnick and Neville, 1997; McConnell, 2002; Sturgess, 1997). However, the number of play assessments was small relative to the volume of research. Furthermore, the assessments were cross-sectional rather than longitudinal and usually applied to pre-school development. Elements of social play were found in a variety of commercially available tests and observation schedules, but the information was fragmented across assessment tools and developmental levels so was time consuming and difficult to extract. The number of items of social play was also limited because these were usually part of an in-depth assessment of another domain, such as pre-verbal communication, pragmatic language or pretend play.

As no specific tool was found for assessing and guiding social play from infancy to adolescence, we set out to develop a method of identifying which children were likely to benefit from intervention, which skills to target and in what order or combination. A prototype was produced and trialled with children aged 3 to 11 years attending an integrated unit for pupils with autistic spectrum disorders within a school for children with moderate learning difficulties. The outcome was that the prototype had potential for identifying pupils' social play skills and needs but that it required a number of modifications. These were made and the SPR began to take shape. A second pilot study undertaken at the school resulted in further improvements. More extensive field trials were then carried out during a two-year research study to refine the SPR and to evaluate its content validity, clinical validity, reliability, generalisibility and acceptability. In all, the three trials involved some 80 children with autistic spectrum disorders, aged from 2 to 15 years. The children represented the range of learning ability and attended a cross-section of mainstream and special education settings.

Thirty parents of children with autistic spectrum disorders worked with the author to develop the parents' questionnaire (the *Home Comments Sheet*). The outcome was a clear mandate on the content of the *Home Comments Sheet* and how it should be used. Interestingly, this matched 'best practice' recommendations in the literature. The *Home Comments Sheet* was positively received by parents in the subsequent evaluation trial: 'It's a great form that caused a lot of thought-provoking!' 'Each question made you think deeply and not skim the surface.'

The research results showed that the Social Play Record was ethically acceptable to children, parents and practitioners, generalised across educational and social settings, and was accessible to users of varying experience. It was sufficiently sensitive to record the progress, however small, of every child in the study. It had theoretical validity, meeting the specifications for a qualitative assessment of social play, and practical application, addressing educational and clinical requirements for formative, diagnostic and evaluative assessment. It provided qualitative information about functional competence and guided intervention (White, 1999, 2002).

The SPR project addressed issues of concern to parents, teachers, therapists and children. It fostered collaboration, which was valued by all participants. Implementing the SPR assessment recommendations not only produced improvements in the children's social competencies per se but also increased their opportunities for social play in two ways. First, parents and practitioners worked together to adapt local play environments, for example, sharing activities (sports, performing arts, play sessions) with other schools and communities; reverse integration, with joint use of specialist facilities (trim track, hydrotherapy pool, sensory room); setting up social clubs; employing play workers to support the children at after-school clubs. Second, parents and practitioners attended joint training on social play, sharing knowledge, developing skills and increasing their confidence and commitment to addressing it.

In summary, the Social Play Record evolved over several years. It originated in response to an unmet need and came to fruition through the active involvement and collaboration of parents, teachers, classroom assistants, speech and language therapists and children. Collectively these individuals shaped and validated the SPR and progressed the work by improving social play opportunities and interventions for local children. It is the sincere wish of all the groups involved in its development that the Social Play Record should be available to anyone working with or caring for children with social interaction needs. However, it is recognised that no tool provides the definitive answer. It is likely that the SPR will undergo further refinements in the light of new knowledge and practical application. Constructive feedback is welcome from anyone using it (see the *Evaluation by Users* form on p.138).

✓

The Social Play Record: A toolkit for assessing and developing social play from infancy to adolescence

EVALUATION BY USERS

The development of the Social Play Record is an ongoing process. Comments and constructive criticisms are welcome.

My evaluation of the Social Play Record is:

Please circle: I have/have not used the Social Play Record.

Date: Designation:

Thank you for your comments. Please return completed form to:

C. White
Gosberton House School
Gosberton
Spalding
Lincolnshire
PE11 4EW
email: c.white510@btinternet.com

References

Alvarez, A., Reid, S. and Hodges, S. (1999) 'Autism and play – the work of the Tavistock autism workshop.' *Child Language Teaching and Therapy 15*, 1, 53–64.

American Psychiatric Association (1994) *Diagnostic and Statistical Manual of Mental Disorders*, 4th edn. Washington, DC: American Psychiatric Association.

Anderson, A, Moore, D, Godfrey, R and Fletcher-Finn, C (2004) 'Social skills assessment of children with autism in free-play situations.' *Autism 8*, 4, 369–385.

Arthur, M., Bochner, S. and Butterfield, N. (1999) 'Enhancing peer interactions within the context of play.' *International Journal of Disability, Development and Education 46*, 3, 367–382.

Asher, S.R. and Hymel, S. (1981) 'Children's social competence in peer relations: sociometric and behavioral assessment.' In G. Wine and M. Smye (eds) *Social Competence in Childhood*. New York: Guildford Press.

Asher, S.R., Singleton, L.C., Tinsley, B.R. and Hymel, S. (1979) 'A reliable sociometric measure for preschool children.' *Developmental Psychology 15*, 4, 443–444.

Attwood, T. (1998) *Asperger's Syndrome: A Guide for Parents and Professionals*. London: Jessica Kingsley Publishers.

Attwood, T. (2000) 'Strategies for improving the social integration of children with Asperger syndrome.' *Autism: International Journal of Research and Practice 4*, 1, 85–100.

Barratt, P., Border, J., Joy, H. and Parkinson, A. (2000) *Developing Pupils' Social Communication Skills: Practical Resources*. London: David Fulton Publishers.

Bauminger, N. (2002) 'The facilitation of socio-emotional understanding and social interaction in high-functioning children with autism: intervention outcomes.' *Journal of Autism and Developmental Disorders 32*, 4, 283–298.

Bauminger, N. and Kasari, C. (2001) 'The experience of loneliness and friendship in autism.' In E. Schopler, N. Yirmiya, C. Shulman and L. Marcus (eds) *The Research Basis for Autism Intervention*. New York: Kluwer.

Bauminger, N. and Shulman, C. (2003) 'The development and maintenance of friendship in high-functioning children with autism: maternal perceptions.' *Autism 7*, 1, 81–97.

Bauminger, N., Shulman, C. and Agam, G. (2003) 'Peer interaction and loneliness in high-functioning children with autism.' *Journal of Autism and Developmental Disorders 33*, 5, 489–507.

Bernard-Opitz, V., Ing, S. and Kong, T. (2004) 'Comparison of behavioural and natural play interventions for young children with autism.' *Autism 8*, 3, 319–333.

Beyer, J. and Gammeltoft, L. (2000) *Autism and Play*. London: Jessica Kingsley Publishers.

Boucher, J. (1999) 'Editorial: interventions with children with autism – methods based on play.' *Child Language Teaching and Therapy 15*, 1, 1–5.

Brown, J. and Whiten, A. (2000) 'Imitation, theory of mind and related activities in autism: An observational study of spontaneous behaviour in everyday contexts.' *Autism 4*, 2, 185–204.

Carpenter, M., Pennington, B. and Rogers, S. (2002) 'Interrelations among social-cognitive skills in young children with autism.' *Journal of Autism and Developmental Disorders 32*, 2, 91–106.

Chandler, S., Christie, P., Newson, E. and Prevezer, W. (2002) 'Developing a diagnostic and intervention package for 2- to 3-year-olds with autism: outcomes of the Frameworks for Communication approach.' *Autism 6*, 1, 47–69.

Charman, T. (1998) 'Specifying the nature and course of joint attention impairment in autism in the preschool years. Implications for diagnosis and intervention.' *Autism: International Journal of Research and Practice 2*, 1, 61–79.

Charman, T. and Baron-Cohen, S. (1997) 'Brief report: prompted pretend play in autism.' *Journal of Autism and Developmental Disorders 27*, 3, 325–333.

Charman, T., Baron-Cohen, S., Swettenham, J., Baird, G., Cox, A. and Drew, A. (2000) 'Testing joint attention, imitation and play as infancy precursors to language and theory of mind.' *Cognitive Development 15*, 4, 481–498.

Corke, M. (2002) *Approaches to Communication Through Music*. London: David Fulton Publishers.

Cumine, V., Leach, J. and Stevenson, G. (2000) *Autism in the Early Years. A Practical Guide.* London: David Fulton Publishers.

Dawson, G. and Osterling, J. (1997) 'Early intervention in autism.' In M. Guralnick (ed.) *The Effectiveness of Early Intervention.* Baltimore, MD: Paul Brookes.

Department for Education and Employment (DfEE) (2000) *Curriculum Guidance for the Foundation Stage.* London: DfEE/QCA Publications.

Department for Education and Skills (DfES) (2001a) *Special Educational Needs: Code of Practice.* London: DfES/QCA.

Department for Education and Skills (2001b) *The Standards Site* (www.standards.dfee.gov.uk/parentalinvolvement/).

Department for Education and Skills and Department of Health (2002) *Autistic Spectrum Disorders: Good Practice Guidance.* Nottingham: DfES Publications.

Department for Education and Skills and Department of Health (2004) *National Service Framework for Children, Young People and Maternity Services: Autistic Spectrum Disorders.* London: DH Publications.

Department of Media, Culture and Sport (2004) *Getting Serious About Play – A Review of Children's Play.* (www.culture.gov.uk/education-and-social-policy/children's-play.htm).

DiSalvo, C. and Oswald, D. (2002) 'Peer-mediated interventions to increase the social interaction of children with autism: Consideration of peer expectancies.' *Focus on Autism and Other Developmental Studies 17,* 4, 198–207.

Frea, W.D. (1995) 'Social-communicative skills in higher-functioning children with autism.' In L.K. Koegel and R.L. Koegel (eds) *Teaching Children with Autism: Strategies for Initiating Positive Interactions and Improving Learning Opportunities.* Baltimore, MD: Paul Brookes.

Frederickson, N.L. and Furnham, A.F. (2001) 'The long-term stability of sociometric status classification: a longitudinal study of included pupils who have moderate learning difficulties and their mainstream peers.' *Journal of Child Psychology and Psychiatry and Allied Disciplines 42,* 5, 592–601.

Frith, U. (1989) *Autism: Explaining the Enigma.* Oxford: Blackwell.

Gray, C. (2002) 'Gray's Guide to Bullying.' *The Morning News 12,* 4.

Guldberg, K. (2001) 'Communication skills in children with autism.' *Special Children 138,* 32–33.

Guralnick, M.J. (1993) 'Developmentally appropriate practice in the assessment and intervention of children's peer relations.' *Topics in Early Childhood Special Education 13,* 3, 344–371.

Guralnick, M.J., Connor, R., Hammond, M., Gottman, J.M. and Kinnish, K. (1996) 'The peer relations of preschool children with communication disorders.' *Child Development 67,* 2, 471–489.

Guralnick, M.J. and Neville, B. (1997) 'Designing early intervention programs to promote children's social competence.' In M. Guralnick (ed.) *The Effectiveness of Early Intervention.* Baltimore, MD: Brookes.

Gutstein, S. and Sheely, R. (2002) *Relationship Development Intervention with Young Children.* London: Jessica Kingsley Publishers.

Gutstein, S. and Whitney, T. (2002) 'Asperger syndrome and the development of social competence.' *Focus on Autism and Other Developmental Studies 17,* 3, 161–171.

Harrison, J. (1998) 'Improving learning opportunities in mainstream secondary schools and colleges for students on the autistic spectrum.' *British Journal of Special Education 25,* 4, 179–183.

Hart, C. (1995) 'Perspectives on autism: what parents want.' In K.A. Quill (ed.) *Teaching Children with Autism: Strategies to Enhance Communication and Socialisation.* New York: Delmar.

Hartrup, W. (1992) 'Friendships and their developmental significance.' In H. McGurk (ed.) *Childhood Social Development: Contemporary Perspectives.* Hove, UK: Lawrence Erlbaum Associates Ltd.

Hepler, J.B. (1997) 'Social development of children: the role of peers.' *Social Work in Education 19,* 4, 242–255.

Hobson, R. (1993) *Autism and the Development of Mind.* Hove, UK: Lawrence Erlbaum Associates Ltd.

Howes, C. (1987) 'Peer interaction of young children.' *Monographs of the Society for Research in Child Development 217,* 53, 1–94.

Howes, C. (1996) 'The earliest friendships.' In W. Bukowski, A. Necomb and W. Hartrup (eds) *The Company They Keep: Friendships in Childhood and Adolescence.* Cambridge: Cambridge University Press.

Howes, C. and Matheson, C. (1992) 'Sequences in the development of competent play with peers: social and social pretend play.' *Developmental Psychology 28,* 5, 961–974.

Howlin, P. (1998) *Children with Autism and Asperger Syndrome: A Guide for Practitioners and Carers.* Chichester: Wiley.

Howlin, P., Baron-Cohen, S. and Hadwin, J. (1999) *Teaching Children with Autism to Mind-Read: A Practical Guide.* Chichester: Wiley.

Howlin, P., Marwood, L. and Rutter, M. (2000) 'Autism and developmental receptive language disorder: a follow-up comparison in early adult life II: social, behavioural and psychiatric outcomes.' *Journal of Child Psychology and Psychiatry 41,* 5, 561–578.

REFERENCES

Hurley-Geffner, C. (1995) 'Friendships between children with and without developmental disabilities.' In L.K. Koegel and R.L. Koegel (eds) *Teaching Children with Autism: Strategies for Initiating Positive Interactions and Improving Learning Opportunities.* Baltimore, MD: Paul Brookes.

Ingersoll, B., Schreibman, L. and Tran, Q. (2003) 'Effect of sensory feedback on immediate object imitation in children with autism.' *Journal of Autism and Developmental Disorders 33*, 6, 673–683.

Jackson, C., Fein, D., Wolf, J., Jones, G., Hauck, M., Waterhouse, L. and Feinstein, C. (2003) 'Responses and sustained interactions in children with mental retardation and autism.' *Journal of Autism and Developmental Disorders 33*, 2, 115–121.

Jarrold, C. (2003) 'A review of research into pretend play in autism.' *Autism 7*, 4, 379–390.

Jarrold, C., Boucher, J. and Smith, P. (1993) 'Symbolic play in autism: A review.' *Journal of Autism and Developmental Disorders 23*, 2, 281–305.

Jones, E. and Carr, E. (2004) 'Joint attention in children with autism: theory and intervention.' *Focus on Autism and Other Developmental Studies 19*, 1, 13–26.

Jordan, R.R. (2003) 'Social play and autistic spectrum disorders: a perspective on theory, implications and educational approaches.' *Autism 7*, 4, 347–360.

Jordan, R.R. and Jones, G. (1999) *Meeting the Needs of Children with Autistic Spectrum Disorders.* London: David Fulton Publishers.

Jordan, R.R., Jones, G. and Murray, D. (1998) *Educational Interventions for Children with Autism: A Literature Review of Recent and Current Research.* Sudbury: DfEE Publications.

Jordan, R.R. and Libby, S. (1997) 'Developing and using play in the curriculum.' In R.R. Jordan and S. Powell (eds) *Autism and Learning: A Guide to Good Practice.* London: David Fulton Publishers.

Jordan, R.R. and Powell, S. (1995) *Understanding and Teaching Children with Autism.* Chichester: Wiley.

Kunce, L. and Mesibov, G. (1998) 'Educational approaches to high-functioning autism and Asperger Syndrome.' In E. Schopler and G. Mesibov (eds) *Asperger Syndrome or High-Functioning Autism?* New York: Plenum Press.

Lawson, W. (2001) *Understanding and Working With the Spectrum of Autism: An Insider's View.* London: Jessica Kingsley Publishers.

Le Couteur, A. (2003) *National Autism Plan for Children (National Initiative for Autism: Screening and Assessment).* London: National Autistic Society.

Lewis, A. (1996) 'Assessment.' In B. Carpenter, R. Ashdown and K. Bovair (eds) *Enabling Access.* London: David Fulton Publishers.

Lewis, V. (2003) 'Play and language in children with autism.' *Autism 7*, 4, 391–399.

Lord, C. (1995) 'Facilitating social inclusion: Examples from peer intervention programs.' In E. Schopler and G. Mesibov (eds) *Learning and Cognition in Autism.* New York: Plenum Press.

Lord, C. and Magill, J. (1989) 'Methodological and theoretical issues in studying peer-directed behaviour and autism.' In G. Dawson (ed.) *Autism: Nature, Diagnosis and Treatment.* London: Guilford Press.

Lord, C. and Magill-Evans, J. (1995) 'Peer interactions of autistic children and adolescents.' *Development and Psychopathology 7*, 611–626.

McConnell, S. (2002) 'Interventions to facilitate social interaction for young children with autism: review of available research and recommendations for educational intervention and future research.' *Journal of Autism and Developmental Disorders 32*, 5, 351–372.

Malone, D. (1999) 'Contextual factors informing play-based program planning.' *International Journal of Disability, Development and Education 46*, 3, 307–324.

Malone, D. and Langone, J. (1999) 'Teaching object-related play skills to preschool children with developmental concerns.' *International Journal of Disability, Development and Education 46*, 3, 325–336.

Malvy, J., Roux, S., Zakian, A., Debuly, S., Sauvage, D. and Barthelemy, C. (1999) 'A brief clinical scale for the early evaluation of imitation disorders in autism.' *Autism: International Journal of Research and Practice 3*, 4, 357–369.

Mesibov, G., Adams, L. and Klinger, L. (1997) *Autism: Understanding the Disorder.* New York: Plenum Press.

Mesibov, G. and Shea, V. (1996) 'Full inclusion and students with autism.' *Journal of Autism and Developmental Disorders 26*, 337–346.

Moyles, J.R. (1994) *The Excellence of Play.* Buckingham: Open University Press.

Mundy, P. and Crowson, M. (1997) 'Joint attention and early social communication: implications for research on intervention with autism.' *Journal of Autism and Developmental Disorders 27*, 6, 653–676.

Nesdale, E. and Flesser, D. (2001) 'Social identity and the development of children's group attitudes.' *Child Development 72*, 2, 506–517.

Odom, S., Brown, W., Frey, T., Karasu, N., Smith-Canter, L. and Strain, P. (2003) 'Evidence-based practices for young children with autism: contributions for single-subject design research.' *Focus on Autism and Other Developmental Studies 18,* 3, 166–175.

Orsmond, G., Krauss, M. and Seltzer, M. (2004) 'Peer relationships and social recreational activities among adolescents and adults with autism.' *Journal of Autism and Developmental Disorders 34,* 3, 245–256.

Overton, S. and Rausch, J. (2002) 'Peer relationships as support for children with disabilities: An analysis of mothers' goals and indicators for friendship.' *Focus on Autism and Other Developmental Studies 17,* 1, 11–29.

Parten, M.B. (1932) 'Social Participation Among Pre-school Children.' *Journal of Abnormal and Social Psychology 27,* 243–269.

Receveur, C., Lenoir, P., Desombre, H., Roux, S., Barthelemy, C. and Malvy, J. (2005) 'Interaction and imitation deficits from infancy to 4 years of age in children with autism.' *Autism 9,* 1, 69–82.

Roeyers, H. and van Berckelaer-Onnes, I. (1994) 'Play in autistic children.' *Communication and Cognition 27,* 3, 349–360.

Rogers, S. (1998) 'Neuropsychology of autism in young children and its implications for early intervention.' *Mental Retardation and Developmental Disabilities Research Reviews 4,* 104–112.

Rogers, S. (2000) 'Interventions that facilitate socialization in children with autism.' *Journal of Autism and Developmental Disorders 30,* 5, 399–409.

Rubin, K. (2002) *The Friendship Factor.* New York: Plenum Press.

Rutherford, M. and Rogers, S. (2003) 'Cognitive underpinnings of pretend play in autism.' *Journal of Autism and Developmental Disorders 33,* 3, 289–302.

Sainsbury, C. (2000) *Martian in the Playground.* Bristol: Lucky Duck.

Schuler, A. (2003) 'Beyond echoplaylia: promoting language in children with autism.' *Autism 7,* 4, 455–469.

Schuler, A. and Wolfberg, P. (1999) 'Peer socialisation and play: the art of scaffolding.' In B. Prizant and A. Wetherby (eds) *Language Issues in Autism and Pervasive Developmental Disorder: A Transactional Developmental Perspective.* Baltimore, MD: Paul Brookes.

Sherratt, D. and Peter, M. (2002) *Developing Play and Drama in Children with Autistic Spectrum Disorders.* David Fulton Publishers.

Sigman, M. (1998) 'Change and continuity in the development of children with autism.' *Journal of Child Psychology and Psychiatry and Allied Disciplines 39,* 6, 817–827.

Sigman, M. and McGovern, C. (2005) 'Improvement in cognitive and language skills from preschool to adolescence in autism.' *Journal of Autism and Developmental Disorders 35,* 1, 15–23.

Siller, M. and Sigman, M. (2002) 'The behaviours of parents of children with autism predict the subsequent development of their children's communication.' *Journal of Autism and Developmental Disorders 32,* 2, 77–89.

Stahl, L. and Pry, R. (2002) 'Joint attention and set-shifting in young children with autism.' *Autism 6,* 4, 383–396.

Stevahn, L., Johnson, D., Oberle, K. and Wahl, L. (2000) 'Effects of conflict resolution training integrated into a kindergarten curriculum.' *Child Development 71,* 3, 772–784.

Strain, P. and Schwartz, I. (2001) 'ABA and the development of meaningful social relations for young children with autism.' *Focus on Autism and Other Developmental Disabilities 16,* 2, 120–128.

Sturgess, J.L. (1997) 'Current trends in assessing children's play.' *British Journal of Occupational Therapy 60,* 9, 410–414.

Tassé, M. and Lecavalier, L. (2000) 'Comparing parent and teacher ratings of social competence and problem behaviors.' *American Journal on Mental Retardation 105,* 4, 252–259.

Terpstra, J., Higgins, K. and Pierce, T. (2002) 'Can I play? Classroom-based interventions for teaching play skills to children with autism.' *Focus on Autism and Other Developmental Disabilities 17,* 2, 119–127.

Tilstone, C. (1998) *Observing Teaching and Learning. Principles and Practice.* London: David Fulton Publishers.

Travis, L., Sigman, M. and Ruskin, E. (2001) 'Links between social understanding and social behavior in verbally able children with autism.' *Journal of Autism and Developmental Disorders 31,* 2, 119–130.

Trevarthen, C. and Aitken, K. (2001) 'Infant intersubjectivity: research, theory and clinical applications.' *Journal of Child Psychology and Psychiatry and Allied Disciplines 42,* 1, 3–48.

Trevarthen, C., Aitken, K., Papoudi, D. and Robarts, J. (eds) (1996) *Children with Autism: Diagnosis and Interventions to Meet their Needs.* London: Jessica Kingsley Publishers.

United Nations (1959) *Declaration of the Rights of the Child.* UN.

van Berckelaer-Onnes, A. (2003) 'Promoting early play.' *Autism 7,* 4, 415–423.

Vygotsky, L. (1978) *Mind in Society: The Development of Higher Psychological Processes.* Cambridge, MA: Harvard University Press.

Weitzman, E. (1992) *Learning Language and Loving It.* Toronto: Hanen Centre Publications.

White, C.A.M. (1999) *The Social Play Record©.* Unpublished work.

REFERENCES

White, C.A.M. (2002) 'The Social Play Record: the development and evaluation of a new instrument for assessing and guiding the social interaction of children with autistic spectrum disorders.' *Good Autism Practice 3*, 1, 63–78.

Widgit Software Ltd. (2000) *Writing with Symbols.* Cambridge: Widgit Software Ltd.

Williams, D. (1992) *Nobody Nowhere: The Extraordinary Autobiography of an Autistic.* New York: Times Books.

Williams, D. (1996) *Autism: An Inside-out Approach.* London: Jessica Kingsley Publishers.

Williams, E. (2003) 'A comparative review of early forms of object-related play and parent–infant play in typical infants and young children with autism.' *Autism 7*, 4, 361–374.

Williams, E., Costall, A. and Reddy, V. (1999) 'Children with autism experience problems with both objects and people.' *Journal of Autism and Developmental Disorders 29*, 5, 367–378.

Williams, E., Reddy, V. and Costall, A. (2001) 'Taking a closer look at functional play in children with autism.' *Journal of Autism and Developmental Disorders 31*, 1, 67–77.

Williams, J., Whiten, A. and Singh, T. (2004) 'A systematic review of action imitation in autistic spectrum disorder.' *Journal of Autism and Developmental Disorders 34*, 3, 285–299.

Wimpory, D., Hobson, R., Williams, J. and Nash, S. (2000) 'Are infants with autism socially engaged? A study of recent retrospective parental reports.' *Journal of Autism and Developmental Disorders 30*, 6, 525–536.

Wing, L. (1996) *The Autistic Spectrum: A Guide for Parents and Professionals.* London: Constable.

Wolfberg, P. (1995) 'Enhancing children's play.' In K. Quill (ed.) *Teaching Children with Autism.* London: International Thomson Publishing.

Wolfberg, P. (1999) *Play and Imagination in Children with Autism.* New York: Teachers College Press.

Wolfberg, P. (2005) *Peer Play and the Autistic Spectrum.* Chesterfield: Winslow Press.

Wolfberg, P. and Schuler, A. (1999) 'Fostering peer interaction, imaginative play and spontaneous language in children with autism.' *Child Language Teaching and Therapy 15*, 1, 41–52.

Wood, M. (1995) 'Parent–professional collaboration and the efficacy of the IEP process.' In L.K. Koegel and R.L. Koegel (eds) *Teaching Children with Autism: Strategies for Initiating Positive Interactions and Improving Learning Opportunities.* Baltimore, MD: Paul Brookes.

Zanolli, K., Daggett, J. and Adams, T. (1996) 'Teaching pre-school age autistic children to make spontaneous initiations to peers.' *Journal of Autism and Developmental Disorders 26*, 407–422.

Zercher, C., Hunt, P., Schuler, A. and Webster, J. (2001) 'Increasing joint attention, play and language through peer supported play.' *Autism 5*, 4, 374–398.